# GRACE

## ROD PARSLEY

CHARISMA
HOUSE

Most CHARISMA HOUSE BOOK GROUP products are available at special quantity discounts for bulk purchase for sales promotions, premiums, fund-raising, and educational needs. For details, write Charisma House Book Group, 600 Rinehart Road, Lake Mary, Florida 32746, or telephone (407) 333-0600.

GRACE by Rod Parsley
Published by Charisma House
Charisma Media/Charisma House Book Group
600 Rinehart Road
Lake Mary, Florida 32746
www.charismahouse.com

Visit the author's website at www.rodparsley.com.

Library of Congress Cataloging-in-Publication Data:
Names: Parsley, Rod, author.
Title: Grace / Rod Parsley.
Description: Lake Mary, FL : Charisma House, 2018. | Includes
bibliographical references.
Identifiers: LCCN 2018029869 (print) | LCCN 2018032453
(ebook) | ISBN
9781629996028 (ebook) | ISBN 9781629996011 (trade paper)
Subjects: LCSH: Grace (Theology) | Law (Theology)
Classification: LCC BT761.3 (ebook) | LCC BT761.3 .P26 2018
(print) | DDC
234--dc23
LC record available at https://lccn.loc.gov/2018029869

18 19 20 21 22 — 10987654321
Printed in the United States of America

# Contents

# A People of Law and Grace

H E NEVER INTENDED to be here. How could the road which seemed so broad and bright just a few months before lead from where he had been to where he was now? Was it a dream? That was impossible. Dreams never had the elements that surrounded him. Nightmares, yes; but he was already wide awake. As benumbed as he was from lack of food and sleep, his mind couldn't avoid recalling the events that had led to his present and deplorable state of affairs.

He was the younger son in a family that was respected throughout the community. His life was characterized by promise. His parents had already made many of the sacrifices that often accompany young married people finding their way and establishing a business, and by the time he came along, they were living quite comfortably. By all accounts, his life should have turned out exceptionally well. *Potential* was the word he heard most often from his parents, teachers, and others. True enough, he had an abundance of potential—a good family name, a strong physique, a pleasing voice, intelligence, ambition—in other words, everything that spelled success in life simply waiting to be realized.

But somehow, something went terribly wrong. Try

as he might, he couldn't identify one specific incident that caused him to turn aside from the life he had known. However, there were a number of indicators that collectively should have warned him of his departure from and disinterest in the things his parents had taught him with their words and modeled in him with their lives. He went from being a compliant child to a contrary kid. He began purposefully to do the opposite of what was expected. When directed to go right, he wanted to go left. He much preferred talking to listening. Naturally, he chose the company of like-minded friends and avoided the influence of mature mentors. Idleness appealed to him much more than industry. Worldly entertainment demanded his time and attention. His needs, his desires, and his claims had priority over everyone else's. Anger and rebellion replaced peace and obedience.

Above all, he demanded the freedom to make his own choices, have his own way, and live his life without regard to any rules or regulations that would restrict his indulgence and pleasure. He chided that his family was just too old-fashioned, too out of step with the times. They didn't and couldn't possibly understand him. They were bound by laws and traditions which he rejected summarily. He would not be chained to a life of perceived drudgery working in the family business.

Finally, the crisis came when he directed one of his increasingly frequent outbursts of anger toward his mother. When his father intervened, he rejected any accountability for his actions and announced that he was leaving home. He demanded the finances that had been set aside for his future—and to his surprise, his father gave it to him—all of it. He declared that he wanted and deserved his freedom, and now he had it. He intended to use it. The world was calling, and he was determined to answer.

Without delay he headed to the largest, most cosmopolitan place he could find. He filled his days and nights with gambling, drinking, dancing, and every other diversion the culture had to offer. Finally, he had everything he desired—fun, freedom, friends, and other pleasures that promised to bring him the fulfillment he craved. There was always something new, something more exotic, something more desirable that would surpass the excitement he experienced the day before. It seemed as though the rollick and frolic would never end.

Until it did. His spendthrift ways, poor choices, false friends, bad investments, and deficient discipline landed him on the street in an incredibly short period of time. He forgot there would be a payday. He found himself with himself—alone. He had no home, no money, no prospects, no joy or peace, and no hope. Those he called his friends refused to speak to him. He had no work history and few marketable skills. His life was in free fall, and landing at the bottom was especially hard for him. He finally found work, as unsuited to it as he was, at a farm where the owner asked no questions about his background.

It could not be called a life—he was barely scratching out the most meager of existences. Before long he was shoeless and shirtless, sleep deprived and starving. He was cold and filthy, desperately lonely and perpetually hungry. Hunger is a more powerful motivator than pride. The startling realization was apparent: this was not life but a slowly progressing death. If he remained where he was, he would die.

Going home to family was the only reasonable choice. It would mean humbling himself, facing his father, and admitting to him how desperately wrong he had been. He would also beg for any kind of job that would enable him to have so much as a morsel of bread. It necessitated immediate departure while physical strength for the long journey was still available.

You may already be familiar with this story that Jesus told about the prodigal son, recorded by Luke in the fifteenth chapter of the Gospel that bears his name. But whenever this parable is preached, the emphasis is almost always on the son who left home. I like to point out that the story begins with Jesus saying, "A man had *two* sons."[1] The behavior of the younger of the two represents to us the excesses of the false grace doctrine that is attempting to make its way through the body of Christ. (A gift as great as God's grace toward man should be emphasized in our preaching and in our thinking. But proper emphasis is far removed from the perversion of doctrine that is being promoted in some religious circles today.) But what of the older son—the one who remained at home? What might be learned from him?

Jesus did not tell stories to pass the time but to make a point. I believe the Lord Jesus' inclusion of the older son's attitude and actions in this parable reveals something about the excessive adherence to religious law-keeping that is also negatively impacting the modern church.

The passage continues, "So he divided his estate between *them*."[2] It wasn't just the younger son who had access to his inheritance—both sons were given their portion of the family fortune. Nothing further is of record regarding the older son until the prodigal comes home and the father throws a party to celebrate his arrival. Instead of the older brother being happy, he becomes angry and refuses to join the celebration. He has a self-righteous attitude, accuses his father of being unfair, and despises his younger brother. I see a similar response by the religious legalists of our day when someone who doesn't meet their approval returns to our heavenly Father.

The younger son was separated from his father by demanding his rights and forsaking his responsibilities. But the older son was also separated from his father by demanding that everyone else meet standards that his father never required. The younger son had a party every day until he ran out of money. The older son never had a party (although he could have had one whenever he wanted) and didn't think anyone else should either—for any reason—even if someone came back from the grave.

Neither excesses of false grace nor excesses of religious law caused them to conform to their father's desires. Both sons were out of fellowship with their father and did not know their father's heart, nor had they any interest in his plans for them. The younger son did not understand that freedom's purpose was to fulfill the father's will. The older son thought that all the father wanted was more and more work, without regard to their relationship. One son was estranged while far from home, and the other was estranged while he was in the home. One came to know bondage to another man's rules, while the other was in bondage to his own rules. Both of them were in grievous error.

Let me explain the danger in the doctrines of false grace and legalism another way, using the same parable of the prodigal son. The clamorous controversy between supposed diametrically opposed extremes of law and grace circulating in much of today's evangelical church can be illustrated very simply by examining the distinction between slavery and sonship.

A slave must follow written ordinances that are

often harshly enforced and result in a culture of fear and punishment. This was certainly true in first-century Judea and throughout much of the rest of the Roman Empire. As I wrote in *The Cross*, "crucifixion actually began not as a form of execution but as a form of punishment. It was designed as...torture...used on...slaves...to terrify the rest of the enslaved populace into compliant servitude."[3]

God recorded His law in the form of ten commandments given supernaturally to Moses on Mount Sinai. Those laws tell us, among other things, not to kill, steal, or covet. God did not give these laws to restrict men but to free them from the impulses that would lead them to certain death and destruction. But what happens so often is that God's ten laws morph and multiply into thousands of man-made laws that do nothing but constrain people. This is the essence of religious bondage. We've all heard of or experienced such religious legalism in some form. It can readily be described as the culture of no and can't, a system of rules and regulations. And as a result, a loving God becomes depicted as an angry and evil tyrant willing to cut off anyone who enjoys any measure of freedom at all. God forbid that we should fall into the error of thinking that pleasing God is only about slavish conformity concerning external appearances and actions. Holiness is and has always been, first and foremost, a matter of our hearts being submitted to the living Christ by the power of the Holy Spirit.

A son, on the other hand, serves not based on obligation enforced by fear but willingly, from the heart, because of love, respect, admiration, and appreciation. Sons can often be identified by their outward appearance. This is certainly not unusual, and all of us have probably heard this phrase or something similar about a child's face or other features: "Oh, he looks just like his father!" However, even if a son does not look like his father outwardly, he will surely have some characteristics of his father that show up in other ways. In fact, a son who does not look like his father, who does not have any of the mannerisms of his father, and who behaves completely the opposite of his father may face suspicion about whether he is actually related at all!

Unfortunately, there are those who would maintain that a son has no responsibility to serve anyone but himself. The prodigal son in the parable of Luke 15 had that attitude. He demanded his inheritance, took it, and "wasted his substance with riotous living."[4] And sonship soon became slavery.

Some might protest and shout, "Yes, he became a slave who was feeding the hogs." But I maintain that he became a slave long before he found himself in that hog pen. The Book of Romans says, "Don't you realize that grace frees you to choose your own master? But choose carefully, for you surrender yourself to become a servant—bound to the one you choose to obey. If you choose to love sin, it will become your master, and it will own you and reward you with death. But if you choose to love and obey God, he will lead you into perfect righteousness."[5]

The prodigal's inheritance was intended to provide and perpetuate a blessing for himself, his family, and many others in future years. The responsible and right course of action for him would have been to manage it wisely and use it to that end. Instead, the prodigal did what many who advocate a false and cheap version of God's grace do today—he took the manifold blessing of God and squandered it on himself, the desires of his flesh, and the pride of life![6] Of course, they become slaves in the process.

That prodigal lost everything—even his self-respect—and became indistinguishable from his surroundings. He did not influence the culture, but the culture certainly influenced him. He lived with hogs, he was as dirty as hogs are dirty, and he smelled like hogs smell. In some respects he was worse off than the hogs—they were full, and he was empty; they were fulfilling their purpose, but he was in no way fulfilling his. He eventually came to the realization and revelation that his father's slaves were better off than he was.

My purpose is to help you avoid either of these extremes—being bound by legalism on one hand, or on the other hand, being bound by a false and cheap version of God's unparalleled and powerful grace.

One of the reasons for my concern is that we are a generation that seems to be given to extremes. Our culture tends to separate people into divisions and then convinces them that they are in competition with each other for the same limited resources. In addition, the anonymity of electronic communication affords us the luxury of throwing bombs and bricks, insults and verbal attacks at one another with impunity. Not only can we not agree, we can't even agree to disagree. Those with differing opinions are no longer friends to be debated but enemies to be destroyed. The concepts of subtlety and sensitivity, and the ability to recognize that truth is often in the tension between two ideas, appear to be lost on our age. We are addicted to hard lines of one kind or another. We don't seem to be comfortable at the intersection of truths. Somehow we've become persuaded that truth is only found at opposite ends of the ideological spectrum, and it has made us a contentious, divided, exhausted, and unwise generation. The novelist F. Scott Fitzgerald once wrote, "The test of a first-rate intelligence is the ability to hold two opposing ideas in mind at the same time and still retain the ability to function."[7] Sadly, he wasn't describing today's generation.

This is at the heart of our current crisis of law and grace. Scripture calls us both to walk in the grace of

God and to be guided by the standards of God—the boundaries that prescribe His will for our lives. This is what pleases Him. This is what makes us holy, keeps us in the power of the Spirit, and makes us an answer to the crying needs of this hurting world and bewildered generation. Unfortunately, many Christians take mindless refuge in one extreme or the other. They either live a brand of grace that makes their lives barely distinguishable from the lives of those trapped in this fallen, self-centered, and lascivious culture, or they bind themselves to an ever-growing list of laws, rules, and regulations, most of which have nothing to do with the will of God expressed in His Word. The saddest aspect of this reality is that between believers living in complete license and carnality and believers living in the dusty death of religious regulations, we're becoming a laughingstock. We are also weak and divided, allowing the lost souls of our generation to plummet to hell while we're distracted defending our excesses.

To illustrate this further, following are two quotes from well-known writers who hail from opposite sides of the controversy.

> Christians are truly free. We are free to laugh or cry, read a novel or the Bible, eat meat offered to idols or avoid it, drink wine or water, smoke or chew, get fat or fit, attend church or stay at home,

tithe or give nothing—all without condemnation from God.[8]

The Christian life...must be a law-formed life....Though believers must not try to keep God's law as a means of earning their salvation, they are nevertheless enjoined to do their best to keep the law as a means of showing their thankfulness to God for the salvation they have received as a gift of grace.[9]

Unfortunately, we are experiencing many variations on these themes. There are religiously superstitious extremes afoot that are as damaging as any other form of error. I encounter this incessantly. For instance, a lady and her husband invited me to dinner after a meeting. As we approached the restaurant, the woman suddenly and quite dramatically put her hand in front of me as if I was about to bound over a cliff.

"Oh, we can't go in there," she gasped, as though she'd seen a ghost. My response was a bewildered, "Why not?" I was hungry! She had discovered a statue in the lobby of the establishment. I just gazed right back at her as though to say, "Seriously? So what!" My hungry belly and I were in no mood for her next religious rhetoric. "Oh, that represents Satan, Satan—I tell you, Satan!" She was all but hissing like a serpent herself.

So I responded in kind, "You mean to tell me I can't go in here and have a deliciously juicy and thick steak simply because there's a cheap concrete statue with a broken ear crouched in a corner of the waiting area?" Her immaturity was on open display. She was saying that even though we are washed in the blood of Jesus Christ and the same Spirit that raised up Christ from the dead dwells within us, He was no match for that concrete statue.

You see, this lady was confused about law and grace—about what could or should be done that was pleasing to God. I could relate more stories to you that are even worse. I'm sure you have some of your own. It seems that individual believers and the body of Christ as a whole are being torn apart by extremes of law and grace. A portion of the responsibility for this spiritual disorientation is the way our modern pleasure-addicted society emits a magnetic pull upon our souls. Another contributor is the lack of solid biblical teaching in our modern churches. There is also the sad fact that many Christians think it is their gift to judge the Bible rather than to allow the Bible to judge them. So they pick and choose what they decide is convenient for them to adhere to in Scripture and then create unbiblical ideas regarding law and grace as an excuse for whatever behavior they choose to enjoy. Idolatry creates a god who is conducive to and supportive of the lifestyle they have chosen to live—why, just step right up to the spinning wheel of "grace" and choose your reality.

I am compelled to help us all find some biblical

sanity in the pages of this book, but first let me establish two pillars of my own thinking so that you understand my point of view. Please know that I have witnessed some examples of religious legalism in my time. I have watched Christians tie themselves in knots about the laws of God and the laws of men in such extreme ways that I thought they would never recover. I grew up among people who adhered to some forms of legalism, and the college I attended to prepare for the ministry had a holiness background. I know what it is to have the definition of *holiness* become entangled in whether you go to movies, or whether your hems and cuffs are the right length, or whether you wear makeup or cologne. I've even seen holiness measured by how much noise you make in church.

All of this makes me grateful for the amazing grace of the Lord Jesus Christ—grace that is uncovered, unfiltered, and most certainly undeserved. I love Him because He died for me. I love Him because He provided eternal salvation as a free gift by His cross. Let me remind you that the cross is where God's unfathomable love intersects with our deepest and most basic need. I love Him because He first loved me. I love Him particularly because He has not merely set up a religious system of dos and don'ts. But rather, He has called me to a "real religion" of relationship based on love and enhanced with power.

When I hear about the legalistic extremes that

permeate the Christian world, my mind goes back to a song I heard years ago—and it's not even a Christian song. Still, it captures what I start feeling when I hear about legalistic actions of believers toward one another and the world they are called to reach. This song was released as a single by a group called Five Man Electrical Band in 1971, and it had a one word title: "Signs." It spoke very simply but powerfully about the proclivity of human beings to try to limit others by putting up signs.

Perhaps you remember this baby boomer classic. I know that referring to this song will make some folks wonder if I could now even be considered a Christian, much less a preacher. I can just hear them saying, "Oh, that Rod Parsley! He's gone to hell on the wings of demon-inspired rock 'n' roll!" Well, I can't help what they'll say, and I can't help but truly appreciate that song. It was practically the theme song of my generation, and it still touches me. We all love freedom. We all resist legalism and being hemmed in by human laws or a false version of God's laws. What I'm saying is, I get it! Grace is the answer to the human condition, and I have never lost sight of that—and I maintain that truth as foundational and fundamental today.

I also have to say, though, that God's grace—and by this I mean the biblical version—is not a card with "Exempt From All Duty" stamped upon it. The powerful grace of God is not an excuse for relinquishing all obligations to God and our fellow man. It is quite the opposite. The more we become the recipients of His grace, the more we should become overwhelmed with humility in light of such an immeasurable and unspeakable gift, and the more we become eager to honor the God who bestowed it. The more we love the Lord, the more we desire to offer everything to Him in full and complete surrender, not in a vain attempt to earn our salvation by works, but rather to serve in freedom and with great joy for the One who has already earned our salvation: Jesus Christ our Lord.

What seems to have happened in our generation is that some Christians have embarked upon a quest of redesigning and reimagining, reworking and renaming Christianity to make it suitable to their earthly desires. Today in some churches, if the cross is mentioned at all, it's often only to warp its meaning and message into something more palatable to modern sensibility. They make God's grace the basis for doing things Jesus would never do. They receive the grace of God and then happily and blindly give themselves to a lifestyle completely foreign to the nature of the Christ they claim to serve. This sounds arrogant and ungrateful to me. If someone bestows a great gift upon you, the appropriate response is not to use it to do the exact opposite of what would please its giver. Yet this is just what foolish and unreasoned ideas concerning God's grace are moving some Christians to do today.

One of the best phrases I have heard to describe this phenomenon is the term *cheap grace*. It was the great German theologian and activist Dietrich Bonhoeffer who coined this phrase, and I find his writing about this cheap grace to be profound, prophetic, and powerful.

Just listen to these words from his classic work *The Cost of Discipleship*.

> Cheap grace is the grace we bestow on ourselves. Cheap grace is the preaching of forgiveness without requiring repentance, baptism without church discipline, Communion without confession.…Cheap grace is grace without discipleship, grace without the cross, grace without Jesus Christ, living and incarnate.[10]

So the church world finds itself in the crush between a thousand different schemes of legalism and an "if it feels good, it's God's will" brand of Christianity that uses grace as an excuse for disobedience and God's love as an excuse for self-love. I'm reminded of a commercial that features a sweet older lady who uses her living room wall like a Facebook wall. She "posts" pictures of her friends and vacations on a literal wall in her home. When her dear friend, who understands that Facebook is a computer-based social network, tries to tell her, "That's not how any of this works," she shouts, "I unfriend you!" I want to cry aloud to these contemporary Christians, "Neither one of these opposing theories on the spectrum of grace is how any of this works!" And none of this is what Jesus meant when He said that He had both come to set mankind free and not to abolish the law.

There is a delicate mystery here. There is a balance— a narrow way, a chosen path, a highway to heaven forged and paved by grace. It is not the path of pleasure-seeking and self-indulgence, nor is it the path to religious domination and the tyranny of man-made rules. It is the grace of God informed by and protected by the laws of God.

But something else has occurred to me, and I cannot fulfill my responsibility to you without sharing it. This issue is not only a dichotomous one, involving the tyranny of fleshly passions on one hand and the slavery to a multitude of insatiable laws on the other. The question in my mind is this: How will you choose to be bound? On its surface this may seem to be a paradox, since who among us could imagine willingly choosing bondage? But from my study of the Bible, it seems to me that there are three options for every man and woman, boy and girl on this people planet. The first, and the one that so many associate with bondage, is the often thoughtless adherence to the rigors of religious rudiments. It is not difficult to understand how this can lead to slavery. However, the second, choosing freedom for self without regard for the needs of others, will also lead to limitations just as restrictive as any human-forged religious code. But there is a third way—a better way, and a thoroughly biblical one.

God delivered these instructions regarding Hebrew servants: "However, if the servant plainly says, 'I love my master, my wife, and my children. I will not go out free,' then his master will bring him to the judges, then he shall also bring him to the door or to the doorpost, and his master shall bore his ear through with an awl, and he shall serve him forever."[11] There is a love that would constrain a man to forswear his freedom and to devote himself to a lifetime of servitude in a household that is not his own. This kind of love would cause him to hear and to obey every directive given to him and to deny himself in order to help someone else. He would have a hole pierced through his ear to signify that he was a perpetual servant—a slave for life.

This custom continued into the first century and beyond and was denoted by the Greek term *doulos*, which is interpreted "slave." The great apostle Paul refers to himself in this manner in the New Testament. So do Peter, Jude, and John. What these men were declaring was that their servitude was not limited to a specified number of years, or until a debt was fulfilled, or by any other condition. They were servants for life by conviction and calling, not by compulsion or coercion.

With these things in mind, listen to these words of

the psalmist: "Sacrifice and offering You did not desire; You have opened up my ears to listen. Burnt offering and sin offering You have not required."[12] The words "opened up my ears" have a dual meaning. The phrase can mean ears that are open to hear the instruction of God, or ears that have been opened (bored through, in the Hebrew language) to signify a lifetime of voluntary service. The author of the Book of Hebrews attributes these words to Jesus in Hebrews 10:5–6.

The strongest, most powerful example of bondage is not that which stems from addiction to fleshly impulses or from rigorous allegiance to religious codes of behavior. The ultimate expression of being bound is for the cause of love, as when a slave refused to go free because of love for his lord and his family. And of course, the supreme demonstration of such self-sacrificing love was illustrated on the darkest day of human infamy when a suffering Servant allowed sinful men to pierce His hands and feet to two mean, angry, biting beams in the form of a cross that became renowned as the doorway to heaven.

How should we then live in light of such an example? To perhaps ask the question differently, How can we, having become aware of the cross of Christ, give ourselves to a life of wanton disregard for the needs of others, or put men in religious shackles that God does not require? Rather, what we can and must do is no less than emulate the life of Christ, who said to His disciples on the shores of Galilee then, and says to us now, "Follow Me."[13]

Isaac Watts, that God-inspired writer of sacred songs from an earlier age, caught just a glimpse of this truth and penned these words:

> Alas! and did my Savior bleed
> And did my Sov'reign die?
> Would He devote that sacred head
> For such a worm as I?
>
> Was it for crimes that I had done
> He groaned upon the tree?
> Amazing pity! grace unknown!
> And love beyond degree!
>
> Well might the sun in darkness hide
> And shut his glories in,
> When Christ, the mighty Maker died,
> For man the creature's sin.
>
> Thus might I hide my blushing face
> While His dear cross appears,
> Dissolve my heart in thankfulness,
> And melt my eyes to tears.
>
> But drops of grief can ne'er repay
> The debt of love I owe:
> Here, Lord, I give myself away,
> 'Tis all that I can do.[14]

# PART I

# FOUNDATIONS

THIS SUBJECT OF law and grace is vast. Theologians have long pondered it. Great saints have struggled with it. Entire denominations and movements have been formed from disagreements over it. I have no desire to go lightly into this weighty topic. It must be approached with eminent humility, and yet with a sense of unmitigated urgency. To establish a proper foundation, let us begin with some necessary background of the topic. First, I want to relate to you my personal history, including extremes of both law and grace. Perhaps you will see yourself in my story. You will certainly come to understand why this topic is so vital to me. Then, we will confront, as must be done, the cross, which is where any discussion of Christian holiness and sanctification must rightfully begin. I will then take us to that great moment in church history when the doctrine of salvation by faith was restored to us through the Great Reformation. Finally, we shall recount that critical time in the early church when this very issue of law and grace threatened to destroy the faith. These chapters and the stories I share within them will serve as the background for the truths we will explore thereafter. They will set us on a firm foundation for embracing God's truth regarding law and grace.

# CHAPTER 1

# The Spectrum of Law and Grace

*It isn't a matter of being worthy, for no man is worthy! It isn't our perfection or our penitence, or a matter of our labors to reach the place of perfection or worthiness. It is God's grace alone!*

—Kathryn Kuhlman

3

THIS ISSUE OF law and grace is personal to me. I have witnessed firsthand what it is to live in bondage to rules and "getting it right." I've also experienced the devastation that arises from an errant misunderstanding of divine grace washing away all sense of boundaries and restraint. My aspiration in these pages is to declare the biblical truth of God's free gift of powerful grace to those who will but receive it.

I have become known to most of my audience as a preacher associated with the Pentecostal and Charismatic movements, but my early church life consisted of being raised in more traditional denominations, followed by my Christian college experience in yet an entirely different denominational background. I am extremely grateful for the varied beliefs and truths to which I have been exposed over the years. I am thankful for how God used them to help define my life and calling.

I certainly don't claim to know everything about the subject of God's undeserved grace, but it is my sincere desire to uncover the truth of God's Word as it has been revealed to me as we navigate the broad spectrum of opinions on this highly debated matter. In one camp we have those who subscribe to the "greasy grace" doctrine of anything goes; and in the other, those who adhere to a more legalistic persuasion, or "the letter of the law."

Now, those who have never experienced legalism may have difficulty understanding how liberating it is to be free from its shackles. I don't believe in "eternal security" nor do I believe in "unconditional insecurity." Some folks are never secure about going to heaven because they believe that any "bad thing" they ever do, no matter how small, may cause them to slide out of God's hands and right into the fiery palms of Satan. It must be terrifying.

There is one event in particular that I will always remember hearing about as a child that left quite an impression on me.

In 1939 the epic film *Gone With the Wind* was released, and it was eventually distributed to smaller theaters in America. Today I can sit down with my family and appreciate this classic film, yet when it debuted, there was widespread outrage and uproar in many churches because Rhett Butler notoriously used a swear word that begins with the letter *d*. Of course, I'm not advocating the use of profanity, but I live in the real world, and I know how people speak. Frankly, given the filth in most movies today, that one little word in *Gone With the Wind* seems pretty insignificant.

Back then, though, the film industry was held to a much higher standard, and to many Christians of that era it was as if the devil had decided to make movie theaters his home base of operations. When *Gone With the Wind* was scheduled to show, many pastors rose up as though they were preparing to make a last stand against the multiplied minions of hell.

My older family members told me that when the news hit their hometown that *Gone With the Wind* was on its way, the preachers blocked the theater entrances to keep the community from being swept up in Hollywood's evil. That's how worried they were about that one little word in an otherwise landmark movie.

Now, don't get me wrong. I believe in sparing no effort in the pursuit of holiness. Yet hearing about that *Gone With the Wind* episode taught me to fear: "Be afraid! Be very afraid!"

Rather than simply forewarning people about the one off-color word in the movie, the message was, "This movie has a bad word in it that will plant evil in our hearts and in the culture at large. And if we begin to imitate what we see and hear, we will all backslide. Run for the hills. Block the highways. Lock up the children. *Gone With the Wind* is coming to town!"

I know those preachers meant well. Yet when I heard this story recounted around the kitchen table, the unintended message to my young heart was this: sin is more powerful than the grace that saved me. I remember thinking that if one bad word could make so many Christians afraid, and if that one bad word could send us all to hell, then what power did we really have? If we were all going to the hot place because Clark Gable said the d-word, then grace must have a very slippery hold on our lives. The message, then, was that I had better do right or I would squirm out of God's uncertain hold on me and find myself marching in the devil's army.

In short, I had to "do right" to "be right" with God. In fact, the message wasn't just that I had to do *right*. It was that I had better never do *wrong*. Fear is at the heart of all true legalism.

Being reared in church, as a young person I had the propensity to acknowledge God in every situation—which is, of course, a good thing, but as you will see in the following example, it caused me to do some remarkably strange things. For example, when I was in sixth grade, I played Little League baseball. Because I was tall and had a little athletic ability—very little, I realize now—I was my team's pitcher. I hadn't been pitching long when my coach saw something odd about my preparation for each pitch. He noticed that before each windup, I would close my eyes and mumble something. Of course, pitchers shouldn't be closing their eyes while they are on the pitcher's mound. A runner might try to steal a base, or a coach might send a signal. A pitcher with his eyes closed would be blind to all of this. Still, I spent half my time on the mound with my eyes closed.

Finally, my bewildered coach decided he had seen enough. He called a time-out and ran out on the field. "What are you doing, Parsley? Why do you close your eyes for an eternity before every single pitch?" Trust me, he wasn't happy, and he became less so when I answered him.

"I'm praying," I said.

You see, I was convinced that if my eyes weren't closed, then I wasn't really praying, and God wouldn't hear me. The idea that I could pray without moving my lips or with my eyes open just never occurred to me. It is important for me to assure you that the spiritual leaders who shaped my early life were by no means foolish men. They loved God passionately with hearts to please Him. They understood a truth that many in our generation have forgotten: there is power in holiness. We've forgotten today that God is absolutely powerful because He's absolutely holy. He's absolutely holy because He's absolutely pure. He's the only—the only—one God. He's beyond contamination because He's the only one of Him. In His purity is His great power. And so it is with us. When, from a heart of unbridled love, we strive to be pure, holy, and beyond contamination, that's when we are filled with God and with His power.

The problem with so many is that they make regulations for living that aren't actually God's rules. They lose sight of the fact that true holiness is living by faith in the holiness of Jesus Christ, the only sinless human, and not attempting to live a perfect life on our own. We can't. We need Him and the Holy Spirit living through us. In forgetting this truth, many Christians have let religious rudiments replace the value of a transforming experience with God. This leads to the long, slow decline that comes when men's requirements prevail and God's transforming work is absent.

Legalism governs by rules created by men. In true legalistic churches, holiness has been and still is almost entirely a matter of externals. A woman was thought to be loose if her wrists slipped out of her sleeves and too much skin was visible. She was expected to have a collar that went up her neck and peeled outward at her jawbone so that almost nothing of her neck was exposed. Apparently a lady's neck was a particularly potent source of temptation. Makeup was unthinkable, of course. Only a lady of the night wore makeup. I remember my parents telling me that teenaged girls would pinch their cheeks to redden them just before a good-looking boy walked by.

I probably don't even have to mention what damnation came upon someone who had a drink of alcohol or dared to enter a bar or tried out a dance step, even in the privacy of their own home. They were going to hell and there was no doubt. The devil had them in his grip.

It really did get absurd. People were called out and rebuked by name for listening to the radio—"a demon box," it was sometimes called. Women were expected to keep their hair tied up in a bun—"bundage," I later called it—and if that bun came undone in public, it was a sign of loose morals and a dark heart. People talked about it. Even wearing bright colors or a piece of jewelry could set tongues wagging.

These are extreme examples, I know, and it is rare to hear about such legalistic ideas today, but they certainly still exist in some form or fashion. I often wonder how many converts we have lost because they look at the church and its long list of rules and legalities and think they will never measure up. They are handed a religious standard they have no hope of reaching instead of a relationship with the One who fulfilled the rules for us. I can still weep today for the weary ones who never got so much as a sip of grace in their churches. I grieve for the image of God presented to a dying world—to the spiritually hungry, to the addicted, to the unwed mothers, or to those who did such things as smoke a cigarette. They were offered a God who was an angry judge, ready to consume with fire those who committed the smallest offense.

Who would desire to surrender to a God like that?

At the heart of the matter is this: Christianity is about receiving grace from the only person who could be sinless in this world—Jesus Christ. The message of the gospel is not that I can do it if I try hard enough, but that Jesus already did it. There is no effort on my part that could save me, and this is exactly why God sent His one and only Son.

When God gave me a full understanding of the completed work of Jesus Christ at Calvary and the free gift of grace, it transformed me forever. Admittedly, I went from a sometimes fearful person trying to obey all the rules to a person in love with Jesus Christ, infused with the power of the Holy Spirit to walk in the will of God. I turned my focus from "trying not to do the wrong thing" to "living out the right thing."

I understood that I was in a process and was not surprised that I sometimes failed. When I did, I repented. It was what a loving God called me to do. When I repented, fellowship was restored. Power returned. Peace reigned. Love ruled. It was truly amazing grace— grace that is undeserved.

This was far different from what I had previously experienced when I first acknowledged the call of God on my life at age seventeen. I felt I would be out of God's will and fall from grace if I didn't read a certain amount of chapters in my Bible every single night. One evening I fell asleep early and woke up in the middle of the night. Immediately the adversary began to harass me, telling me to get up and read my Bible unless I wanted to suffer the consequences of God being angry with me. With the help of the Holy Spirit, I found the fortitude to tell the devil—and myself—"God loves me whether I read a certain amount of His Word nightly or not, and tonight I refuse to be tormented by you any longer!" I turned over and pillowed my head with the full assurance that God loved me and His grace was sufficient for me.

I have recounted these experiences from my early life to tell you this: I understand what it is for people to be bound in religious tradition and law but also for them to discover freedom in God's grace and mercy. I'm eternally grateful for the Christian truths and values of my upbringing, as well as God's continual revelation of His grace that breaks the chains of human rules, man's expectations, and superstitions. The only purpose they serve is to cause fear and uncertainty, thereby never allowing us to enjoy the precious gift of grace provided by our Father God.

I can honestly tell you that in my youth, I lived a consecrated life. I was dedicated. It is true. I had righteous parents and pastors who were great men and women of God. We were striving to be holy because we wanted to be righteous and we wanted God's power and presence.

What did this look like in my life? I sought God. I wanted to find Him, to know Him, to experience Him, to be changed by Him, to know His ways and His thoughts, and to experience His presence. As the Bible taught me, I sought God in the morning, I sought Him in the evening, and I sought Him at noon too. And I prospered. I don't mean I became materially rich, though I certainly had more than I needed of natural things. What I mean is that I flourished in the biblical sense of that word. I prospered in spirit, soul, and body. I walked in the favor of God, had success at whatever I put my hand to, had wisdom and understanding for living beyond my years, and felt God guiding my life. I read the Bible, meditated on its words, prayed for their meaning, and gave myself to its precepts.

I'm not bragging here. I'm trying to share with you something vitally important. I was not perfect, but I did seek a perfect God. Here's what I came to know. The external worked its way into the internal. My outer life became the gateway for transformation of my inner life. In other words, God took possession of me. I don't mean this in some extreme, robotic sense. I just mean that God indwelt me and began making me His. He changed my desires, my passions, my hopes, my dreams, and my ways. He took over.

You shouldn't be surprised that I say this. All I'm describing is what the Bible tells us will happen. First Peter 2:9 says we are "a chosen generation, a royal priesthood, an holy nation, a peculiar people" (KJV). The literal translation of the word *peculiar* from the original language is "possessed." And this was, in my imperfect way, what I lived—an increasingly God-possessed life.

I experienced the power of God at work in my life transforming my desires. You see, I knew the law of

God. I knew the "dos and don'ts." Like anyone else, I could see what I should do and what I should not do based on God's revealed Word. Yet something deeper and more lasting began happening to me, as it does to everyone who delights themselves in the Lord. My desires changed. My heart aligned. My passion became to do His will. The Holy Spirit was remaking me from within, and He was fashioning me in the image of Jesus.

The glorious reality that freed me from any form of legalism is that boundaries produce freedom. Order produces freedom. This may sound like an oxymoron, but it's like I tell our students at Harvest Preparatory School: Wear your uniform. You'll be free. You won't have to get up in the morning and decide what you're going to wear. And you don't have the peer pressure of looking at what someone else is wearing and seeing that they have something you don't because you don't have the money. You're free of all that because you have order and boundaries in your life. Yes, law brings freedom when it is good law.

Furthermore, grace came to fulfill the law, not destroy it. The law says don't commit adultery. But there is a law of love. It comes with grace and gives me the strength to say, "I'm not going to commit adultery with your wife, because I love you." I don't refuse to sin just because the Bible said I had to. The Bible told me I had to until I was tutored in the law to the point that I realized that it was given for my strength. And in that strength I find freedom.

I hear people say all the time, "Well, the curse of the law…" Let me tell you, dear friend, the curse of the law is not that the law is cursed. The curse is in our inability to keep the law. That's the curse—that we couldn't keep it. I'll go into more detail on this in chapter 3, but a major theme of Martin Luther's reformation was something in the Latin called *sola gratia*. It very simply means by grace alone. Luther preached it loudly and boldly! He preached that grace was extended to sinners as the gift of God. He boldly rejected any notion that anyone could ever be deserving of the grace of God based on their own good works, regardless of what denominational headquarters sanctioned. Grace alone was the foundation of Luther's message. How we need this today.

I've taken all this time to describe my progression in Christ because I want to show you the near opposite that is becoming the norm today. In biblical Christianity you are saved, you are indwelt by the Holy Spirit, you take in the Word of God, and the Holy Spirit begins changing you. You begin to live contrary to the ways of this world and free of the magnetic pull of moral destruction that dominated you before you came to know the Lord. You'll make mistakes and missteps, but you'll rise above them. God declared your victory before you were even born. How grateful we should be!

Yet in our current culture there is a completely different kind of thinking that has taken root in the soil of the modern church. Today a growing number of Christians don't believe that the Holy Spirit needs to rework their desires. They don't see that there is a war for their souls between the kingdom of darkness and the kingdom of God. Instead, they see the whole matter in terms of their own freedom. They conclude that God has set them free to do as they please; therefore, there is no meaningful struggle for control of their own impulses. There is only a war against their own freedom. The battle has become a fight against anything that restrains them from their own pursuits of what seems right to them.

Here are a few examples. I'm aware that there are ministries today that offer dynamic worship services and that host hundreds of young, passionate people. Yet I am also aware—and it brings me great sadness—that during some of these services, there are couples fornicating in the parking lot at the same time. When they have finished their encounters, they return to the service and continue worshipping. They don't think that what they are doing is at odds with what is happening in the adjoining building. They regard the two activities as two sides of the same coin. They imagine that Jesus loves them and wants them to be happy. If that happiness means sex with their partner, then so be it. They will worship Jesus one minute and have a sexual liaison the next. They will feel no tension, no guilt, and no condemnation as they do.

Still yet, other couples in the church think nothing of living together outside the bonds of marriage and even choose to have children and be seen as a family unit, but marriage is never a consideration. Unfortunately, these behaviors often go unnoticed by their pastors who themselves are leading lives that are void of prayer and devotion to the Word. They want to pray for ten minutes and preach for ten hours with little or no kingdom results rather than being like the apostle Peter, who prayed for ten days and preached for ten minutes and witnessed mighty demonstrations of the power of God.

Where is the will of God in all of this? Don't they realize that when we worship God, we worship Someone who has a will and a desire and a way? He has made that way known. Where is any consideration of the counsel of the Holy Spirit or the authority of Scripture?

This is my cry to this generation. What about the example that Jesus gave us of a life of holiness? The Bible plainly tells us: "Stay away from sexual sins."[1] I don't want to hear about your liberty and your freedom and your will. What is the will of the God who saved us? That is my all-consuming interest, and I think it should be the same with any true, biblically informed, Spirit-filled Christian.

I have told my story—and shared other examples to illustrate the opposite perspective from my own—because I believe that they define one of the great battle lines of our generation. I know—because the Bible tells me so, because I experienced it, and because it has worked for millions of Christians—that the same God who saved us is able to change us so we live according to His will. Sadly, this is far from what has become popular. Today many would say that God has saved us and then He has left us to live as we choose. His love makes no demands, comes with no call for change, and is a mandate for nothing more than a stronger grasp on our own preferences. I think there is a higher way. I believe God is calling. And to the licentiousness among Christians in our age, I say that wherever the will of God and the will of man are in conflict, God's will must prevail. Otherwise, there will be chaos leading to ruin—which is an outcome we should all pray that we avoid in the church.

# CHAPTER 2

# Memento Mori

*When Christ calls a man, he bids him come and die.*

—DIETRICH BONHOEFFER

LLOW ME TO tell you a secret. It has been proclaimed boldly for generations. Here it is: the cross is the issue. This is always true. The cross is the heart of the matter, and this is particularly so regarding law and grace and how we should walk out the two.

We can have all the airy theological debates we want, and we can choose sides and have as many good old-fashioned religious fights as seem appropriate, none of which will ever change the truth that once the human soul has glimpsed the meaning of Calvary's cross—once we have seen the Lamb of God scourged and nailed to a crossbeam before a taunting world, and once we allow the reason He endured it all to capture and take hostage our hearts—God's grace and His law cease to be "issues," "conundrums," or "controversies." They are no longer mysteries to ponder or problems to debate. They become gospel truth shouted from our expiring Savior from that angry beam.

His powerful and matchless grace becomes His glorious gift to be received with absolute awe and transcendent wonder—His law becomes a guardrail to gently guide us away from a dangerous boundary line drawn by our loving Father's powerful hand of protection.

Instead of struggling with the law and kicking against the pricks, a correct response is to fall to our knees singing "All Hail the Power of Jesus' Name" and bring forth the royal diadem and crown Him Lord of all— Lord of our thoughts, our desires, our deeds, and our objectives. Rather than submitting to the tyranny of our flesh, we must declare with certainty born of conviction, as did the ancient Israelites, that "my God is king." The very thought of His unspeakable gift and supreme sacrifice should provoke an honest, heartfelt, and humble response of gleeful gratitude and outrageous obedience.

The cross is the issue—the cross ends the debate, for there remains no man or woman who understands the horror and power of that tormented tree who ever walks away eager to reduce or explain away the requirements of a holy God. No one captivated by Calvary yearns to be free from the restraints of a God who sent His Son off to war in the service of His furious love.

The cross is the issue. Earlier generations knew this, and there is much to be gained by a return to the discarded values of the past. Our American Founding Fathers routinely signed their letters or said goodbye to friends with the Latin phrase *memento mori,* which translated means "remember death." It was a way for believers to remind each other of the death of Jesus Christ—a method for friends to provoke one another to noble and holy living by saying, "Remember death."

Remember that you will die. Remember what legacy you hope to leave, what kind of person you will aspire to have become on that final day as you exhale your final breath on earth. Remember death, and live differently because you do.

I preached a message the week after my father's departure from this natural world titled "Consider Death" based on Deuteronomy 32:29, "O that they were wise, that they understood this, that they would consider their latter end!" (KJV). Death, like sin, is the only certain eventuality we all have in common, but no one wants—or is brave enough—to talk or preach about it anymore. We do not look for death, but it searches for us. Death is certain and sudden for all of us, unless Jesus Christ returns in the glorious rapture of His church!

This *memento mori*—"remember death"—is akin to the words in the Book of Hebrews:

> Let us look to Jesus, the author and finisher of our faith, who for the joy that was set before Him endured the cross, despising the shame, and is seated at the right hand of the throne of God. For consider Him who endured such hostility from sinners against Himself, lest you become weary and your hearts give up.[1]

Let's do this now. Let's consider Jesus and ponder the cross He endured. The truths of law and grace will remain blurred and foggy until they are illuminated by the light of Calvary and brought into focus by Calvary's Lamb. We must take a moment and meditate on the suffering our Savior endured on that sacred Friday. There can be no meaningful discussion of how we should live in this world and how law and grace must work in harmony in our lives unless we have a powerful confrontation with that cross.

The cross had always been before Jesus—in front of Him, beckoning Him, calling Him, compelling Him. He had known since before this world was created that He would die horribly at the hands of raging, cursing conspirators. Revelation 13:8 tells us that the Lamb of God was "slaughtered before the creation of the world" (GW). Before all that exists was spoken into being, the Son of God was already sacrificed in the heart of our Father. Hear Paul in Philippians chapter 2:

> Let this mind be in you all, which was also in Christ Jesus, who, being in the form of God, did not consider equality with God something to be grasped. But He emptied Himself, taking upon Himself the form of a servant, and was made in the likeness of men. And being found in the form of a man, He humbled Himself and became obedient to death, even death on a cross.[2]

Our righteous redeemer left the glories of heaven and condescended to this cemetery planet and subjected

Himself to the limitations of human flesh. Here—He came to die. And in a final indignity infinitely far below His station, He subjected Himself to sinful men and allowed them to violently humiliate and crucify Him. All of this was in the heart of God before He stood in darkness and void and shouted, "Let there be light."

The Lord Jesus grew up acknowledging that execution awaited Him. He was constantly the target of one conspiracy or another contrived by His enemies. In Mark 11:18 we see how the scribes and chief priests "looked for a way to kill Him." Again in John 7:1, "He would not walk in Judea, because the Jews were seeking to kill Him."

Mark 14:1 says, "Now the feasts of the Passover and of Unleavened Bread were two days away. And the chief priests and the scribes looked for a way to...secretly... kill Him." Matthew 26:3–4 confirms that "the chief priests, the scribes, and the elders of the people gathered in the palace of the high priest, who was called Caiaphas, and took counsel that they might take Jesus covertly and kill Him."

So He knew. He always knew. The living Christ was under threat of death His entire life knowing His closest friends and confidants would betray Him. Yet He would not back down from His mission to destroy the rule of evil in the world of men and to loose humanity from the domination of sin by breaking the chains that had held Him bound since the rebellion of our pristine parents in the elegant Garden of Eden.

Then came that agonizing final week in Jerusalem. The religious leaders had already decided to kill Him. By the time Jesus finished His last meal with His disciples, the plot was irrevocably set in motion. Guided by the traitor, the officials who sought His life found Him in a secluded garden. There, under the full light of a Passover moon, as alone as any man has ever been, He was apprehended and taken away while the cowards who swore they'd die with Him fled into the night.

What followed is so ghastly that we want to look away, but we dare not if we hope to understand, if we pray for the mystery of law to be unraveled, if we hope to live lives worthy of all He endured. He was blindfolded, mocked, scorned, and ridiculed. He was beaten, His beard yanked from His face—He was spat upon and relegated to solitary confinement in a cold, damp prison dungeon overnight. The next morning, He was sentenced and scourged.

We tend to pass quickly over this matter of scourging, but since it is presented in Scripture as a vital requirement of divine justice as part of our redemption—Peter tells us, quoting Isaiah 53:5, that "by his wounds you have been healed"[3]—we should take a moment to consider it in all its brutality.

The Romans made scourging an art form called the "almost death." The goal was to take the victim to the edge of death without actually killing him. The Roman army kept a cadre of specifically trained soldiers for scourging—specialists, called *lictors*, who used a device called a *flagellum,* an iron or wooden ring with leather straps tied to it. Interwoven into the straps were pieces of jagged bone, rock, or metal, sharpened to a razor's edge.

Scourging was different than the whippings we're familiar with. In whipping, the idea was to lacerate or cut the flesh. In scourging, the goal was not just to cut the flesh, but to tear it, in bleeding shreds and ribbons, from the bone.

The scourge was devised so that the long leather straps would wrap around a man's torso. Then the lictor, skilled in his art, knew when the hard pieces had dug in fully; it was then that he violently pulled the straps away, causing pieces of the victim's body to be ripped away and flung into the air.

Remember that Psalm 22, the great prophetic psalm of Jesus' sufferings, includes the lines "all my bones are on display; people stare and gloat over me"[4] and "roaring lions that tear their prey open their mouths wide against me."[5] Thus a blood-covered, torn, tortured, and barely recognizable Jesus stood before the crowd while they shouted, "Crucify Him! Crucify Him!"

Our suffering Savior was required to carry His heavy crossbeam through the streets of Jerusalem to the place of execution. He faltered and fell. An African named Simon of Cyrene was made to carry the crossbeam for Him. Finally, barely alive, Jesus arrived at Golgotha, a rocky hill so littered with dead men's bones that skulls covered the ground, giving it its name: "the place of the skulls."

Our Lord Jesus Christ was then impaled upon two intersecting beams. Through flesh, nerves, and bones jagged metal spikes were driven. Then the cross was lowered with a hollow thud into the posthole already prepared for it.

Now the true agony of crucifixion was revealed. The Romans had perfected the art. They wanted something slow and ghastly, something public. They wanted to torture a man to pacify free men and warn slaves. They wanted the sufferings to be so shocking that men would never forget.

The evil secret of crucifixion was that it was a method of slow strangulation. His torso became paralyzed. He could draw air in but could not exhale. To breathe, He had to push down on the spikes through His ankles.

For six hours Jesus hung there between heaven and earth, gasping for air and raking His torn flesh against the biting beams of wood. Beyond His agonies of body were the torments He suffered from taking on the sin of the whole world.

All the horror of unregenerate humanity—every rape and child molestation, every murder and theft, every evil deed of every person through all time—was placed upon our sinless Savior. Finally, mercifully, it ended. Jesus said as much: "It is finished."

Oh, there were glories just ahead. His body would rest in the grave for three days and then be raised to life again. Miracles would begin to manifest. Angels would appear. The proclamation of the risen Christ would begin. Soon there would be a Pentecost outpouring of the Spirit of God that would give birth to a movement that would empower His followers to change the world.

Yet let's not hurry too quickly past the cross—it's important. It's more than that disturbing episode—before all the victory began—that modern preachers don't speak of.

When Jesus described the costliness of the Christian life, He said, "If anyone will come after Me, let him deny himself, and take up his cross, and follow Me."[6] Later, Paul said he wanted to know nothing about the church at Corinth "except Jesus Christ and Him crucified."[7]

Then Peter, who clearly did not understand the meaning of the cross before Jesus was crucified, later wrote, "He Himself bore our sins in His own body on the tree, that we, being dead to sins, should live unto righteousness."[8]

There it is! There is the truth that has moved me to describe the horrors of Jesus' sufferings in such detail.

Until we truly confront the cross and identify ourselves with it, we aren't fully finished with sin. Until
the meaning of the cross is imbedded in our souls, the
full meaning of a liberated Christian life cannot be
ours.

Hear Paul:

> I have been crucified with Christ. It is no longer
> I who live, but Christ who lives in me. And the
> life I now live in the flesh, I live by faith in the
> Son of God, who loved me and gave Himself for
> me.[9]

To take on the Christ-life is to be dead to sin. It is to
hate sin, to see it for what it is and turn entirely from it,
not to ignore its reality and penalty. "For the wages of
sin is death, but the gift of God is eternal life through
Jesus Christ our Lord."[10] To be a Christian is to let go
of every evil in this world and to take on the nature of
the One who died for us.

A culture that emphasizes entitlement has no
interest in heaven and no fear of hell. It has no interest
in any kind of life that suggests anything other than
how much they deserve and all they should possess
and obtain. Any message that involves facing opposi-
tion, doing hard work, mention of self-sacrifice or ser-
vanthood, or even enduring delay has little appeal for
people who believe they already deserve everything
and must earn nothing.

Perhaps then you can understand why I am so insistent that no Christian who understands the price of their salvation would spend the rest of their days trying to figure out how to offer as little as possible to Christ and still be a Christian. Instead of saying, "How close to the world can I get and make it to heaven?" we should be saying, "How close to heaven can I get and still remain on earth?" No one who has received life-changing mercy and unbounded love rises from the experience and goes about trying to figure out how much of the language of this destitute world, the practices of this dying generation, the attitudes of a backslidden church, the entertainments of this detestable world, and their connection to this decaying culture they can hang on to and still stay in relationship with God.

If you've been touched by this kind of heaven-sent, life-transforming grace, you know that nothing else compares with it. Your search for the meaning of life has found its fulfillment in a sacrifice nailed to a tree just outside the walls of Jerusalem. You were the ultimate dead man walking—except that you were not sentenced to life behind steel prison bars but to eternity separated from God in a flaming prison called hell. And after your last vestige of hope had taken wings and flown away, a human governor did not commute your life sentence, but the living Savior set you free from a forever sentence of indescribable suffering and unendurable torment. This is the pearl of great price, the end of the quest, the true secret—the ultimate gift and unplumbed depths of His powerful grace.

Those who have had this experience and who know this truth have no desire to cut a deal with the Jesus who suffered the agonies of hell on a cross to set them free. The only proper response is to fall to our knees and weep out our joy and receive a gift we can barely imagine—and then surrender our total lives to the One who loved us enough to die in our place.

The great martyr Jim Elliot, a missionary who died at the hands of an indigenous people he was trying to reach with the gospel, said: "He is no fool who gives what he cannot keep to gain what he cannot lose."[11] This, my friend, is true Christianity.

Please hear me as I state this most solemn fact: this has *everything* to do with the subject of law and grace. We should have our best minds—our best sages and seers, theologians and thinkers, philosophers and poets—help us work through this issue to mine its glories. We will be required to plumb the depths and scale the heights of revelation knowledge and divine wisdom. We will need to navigate through the full scope and meaning of the law of God for those to whom the grace of God has been given in Christ Jesus through the Holy Spirit. It is by no means trivial or trite. The implications are not only life-changing but destiny-altering.

But let us not have a discussion of the claims of Christ upon our lives unless we are first a people fully given to Him. Let's not attempt a conversation about sacred theology unless we are first determined to be a sacred people! Let us not take the great truths of Scripture and make them bartering tools in an attempt to fashion a compromise with this world and its Satan-dominated, self-seeking, self-indulgent, self-aggrandizing, hell-bound culture.

I suspect that we are now seeing a kind of believer who stands at the very edge of Christianity and wonders why he can't put one foot into the world while keeping the other foot in the church. He attempts to straddle the kingdom of God and the kingdom of darkness with a smile on his face—half-righteous and half-worldly, half-Christian and half-whatever-feels-good-at-the-moment. Such a person is not interested in perfecting holiness in the fear of God but in friendship with the world. The apostle James said it this way: "You unfaithful people! Don't you know that love for this evil world is hatred toward God? Whoever wants to be a friend of this world is an enemy of God."[12] I am concerned that this kind of Christian wants to love Jesus privately but publicly live whatever life a perverse culture offers.

So, this modern Christian is only interested in debating the law of God to see how he can circumvent it and surrender himself instead to the trendier fashions of current culture.

I truly wonder if such church attenders have any idea what the cross of Christ exemplifies. I wonder, Have they contemplated for even the briefest of moments the supreme price He paid and what that payment made possible? Do they know what the cost of that immeasurable divine grace summons from us in return and how completely, entirely, and utterly our lives are no longer our own? Do such casual acquaintances of Calvary even begin to comprehend the sovereign rights of King Jesus upon their lives?

I fear for these weakened worship groupies because as sincere as they may be in their quest for the application of God's law, the truth is that many of them have clung to portions of their former, fallen, and failing lives that they simply are not willing to relinquish.

A friend of mine—an official at a major university—received a message that there was an emergency at the sports facility. He rushed there, and when he arrived, he saw a woman screaming as though someone was dying. Her husband was screaming that he was going to sue the university. A little boy was screaming too because his arm was jammed inside of a vending machine.

My friend walked over to the boy and concluded that the child had reached into the machine and somehow become stuck. It was clear from a trickle of blood that something in the machine was cutting him.

So he reached into the machine himself to see if he could get the child free. As he did, he realized the problem. He stood up, looked at the boy, and said, "Son, let go of that candy bar." He did, and his arm slid right out of the machine.

Mom stopped screaming. Dad stopped threatening. That vending machine wasn't devouring the child after all. The boy had simply put a death grip on a candy bar and refused to let go. All that drama simply because he was being denied what he wanted.

In the same way, snowflake Christians have put a death grip on some part of this wretched world, and they simply will not let go. They scream like a child because they aren't getting what they want. Their real problem is that they want what they shouldn't have. They've been bought with a price and belong to someone else. They neither need nor have a right to whatever they're hanging on to so desperately. What they're grasping is the very thing that is destroying them. They are like a man in the middle of the ocean clutching an anchor. He's going to sink. He's going to die holding on to his own destruction.

So I'll preach about how the law of God applies in the light of grace, but not until we fall so in love with Jesus, so tearfully grateful for His cross and so utterly given to Him alone that any claim He lays upon our lives is welcome. I will not preach about the law of God if we're looking for an escape from holiness. Only after we love the cross and submit to its significance can we love God and submit to His divine purpose. Only then will we be joyful travelers on the road of revelation that leads to the fulfillment and purposes of both God's immutable law and His immeasurable grace.

# CHAPTER 3

# Sola Gratia

*A Christian man is the most free lord of all, and subject to none; a Christian man is the most dutiful servant of all, and subject to every one.*

—MARTIN LUTHER

I CAN SPEAK NO further about the glorious grace we have been given in Jesus Christ without speaking of one of the great heroes of the message of divine grace, Martin Luther. How we need people like him today—men and women who understand what it is for the parched, rule-bound, self-loathing, empty soul to be touched by the grace of a loving and eternal God. This is the story of Martin Luther, and I tell it briefly here so that we may remember not only a period in our history but the journey of a great soul from that bondage to spiritual freedom. Perhaps, armed with this story, we can remember also the many souls in need of just such grace today. Perhaps, dear reader and fellow seeker, this may even include you.

Let me say also that rehearsing some of the life history of Martin Luther does not mean that I in any way endorse or agree with all of his writings or attitudes. Luther, especially later in life, expressed an especially virulent and unrelenting anti-Semitism, which is both reprehensible and wrong. None of this, however, changes the significance of the revelation of justification by faith that God gave him and that he gave to the world.

Martin Luther was born in 1483 to a stern, steely

family who lived among a hard and superstition-bound people in Germany. It was an age that forged exceptional men and women, but only if they survived it unmarred and unbroken. Martin Luther was such a man.

Luther was a gifted and highly intelligent child, but he remembered his early years mainly for the harsh parental discipline he endured. He once reported, "My mother caned me for stealing a nut, until the blood came. Such strict discipline drove me to the monastery, although she meant it well."[1] Of his father Luther remembered, "My father once whipped me so that I ran away and felt ugly toward him until he was at pains to win me back."[2]

Still, there was a deep strain of Christianity practiced in the Luther home, and it left its mark on young Martin. Hans, his father, prayed nightly at the bedside of his son that Martin would live pleasing to God. Martin's mother, Margaretta, was a woman of constant, consistent, and fervent prayer, and Martin remembered that weeping voice of supplication and her unending stream of communication with the almighty God for the rest of his life.

Hans Luther was a miner, so the whole family knew well that they must do everything in their power to please St. Anne—according to tradition, the mother of the Virgin Mary—who was the patron saint of miners. This was part of the superstition and unbiblical mysticism that spread over the whole of society. Men labored their whole lives in hope that a saint who ruled their profession might have mercy upon them and give them both safety and success. It was the teaching of the Roman Catholic Church in those days, and it left men subject not only to a scowling God, but also to His unhappy Son, Jesus Christ, and a host of saints whose pleasure must be sought with offerings and prayers in order that one's life might go well.

It was this family's devotion to St. Anne that explains an odd but decisive moment in Martin Luther's life. On a sultry July day in 1505, Luther, then a twenty-one-year-old student at the University of Erfurt, was caught in a violent thunderstorm. When lightning struck near him, he cried out, "St. Anne help me! I will become a monk."[3]

Such a vow was not unusual in that age, but it was unusual for a man like young Martin Luther to feel bound by such a vow, uttered as it was in a moment of extremity. Yet, such was the case, and soon after the storm and the hasty prayer to St. Anne, Martin Luther entered an Augustinian monastery and became a monk. The decision would prove one of the great hinges of history.

What began to unfold from that moment was the struggle of a human soul for peace with the living God. It is important to note that Luther sought this peace in just the way that the Roman Church taught at the time that he should. It would not work for Martin Luther, and we should be glad that it did not, for all of the great truths of faith that came from Luther's life arose from his losing battle to know the living God by means of works.

Like all the monks at the monastery, Luther prayed seven times a day. He was awakened at one in the morning by a bell that summoned him to prayer. He spent his days in intercession, in song, in meditation, and in complete austerity. For another monk, it all might have been the fruit of devotion to God. To Luther, it was an offering to an uncaring God whose pleasure he never seemed to earn.

The truth is that God terrified Luther during these years. Something in Luther's soul made him feel inherently unworthy, and this made every holy duty feel to Luther as though he was reaching out to touch the ark of God only to risk being smitten by holy wrath.

Luther decided to overcome his feelings of rejection by earning the affection of God through works. Few men in all of history have pursued God's love with such utter but legalistic devotion. Luther became like the child who senses the displeasure of his parent and decides to earn that pleasure with gifts and compliments and work.

He began fasting for days on end and did this so often that he eventually ruined his digestive system. He performed more rituals and prayed more prayers than anyone was required to and spent hours lying before the high altar in the cathedral. He believed that the more uncomfortable *he* was, the more comfortable *with* him God might become. He stopped using blankets during the bitter German winter nights and nearly froze to death. He wore clothing of only the roughest cloth to make sure he was miserable nearly every moment. In short, he suffered and labored and sacrificed so that God might turn His smiling face of favor, mercy, and grace toward him.

All his efforts resulted in total and utter failure. It didn't work. It never does. Luther himself admitted as much. Years later he wrote:

> I was a good monk, and I kept the rule of my order so strictly that I may say that if ever a monk got to heaven by his monkery it was I. All my brothers in the monastery who knew me will bear me out. If I had kept on any longer, I should have killed myself with vigils, prayers, reading, and other work.[4]

Luther's search for divine approval through works became absurd. Hoping to confess every single sin he might ever have committed, he once confessed to an older priest for six hours straight. His mentor finally could take it no more. "Look here," he said, "if you expect Christ to forgive you, come in with something to forgive—[the killing of a parent], blasphemy, adultery—instead of all these [trifles]."[5] The truth is, Luther was miserable, and he was making everyone around him miserable as well with his clumsy, extreme, legalistic, overreaching pursuit of a God he thought was angry with him.

In reality Martin Luther was angry with God. As he wrote later:

> Is it not against all natural reason that God out of his mere whim deserts men, hardens them, damns them, as if he delighted in sins and in such torments of the wretched for eternity, he who is said to be of such mercy and goodness? This appears iniquitous, cruel, and intolerable in God, by which very many have been offended in all ages. And who would not be? I was myself more than once driven to the very abyss of despair so that I wished I had never been created. Love God? I hated him![6]

These last three words were the heart of the matter. Luther was angry with God for rejecting him. His mentors at the university thought they knew what he needed. He should go on to earn his doctorate in theology. Perhaps his anger with God would dissolve if he studied God more deeply. Luther was aghast at the suggestion and stammered out a dozen reasons it would never work. The load of the work alone would kill him, he protested. His mentor, an astute man named Staupitz, merely said, "Quite all right. God has plenty of work for clever men to do in heaven."[7] Clearly, Staupitz was as weary of Luther's excesses as everyone else was.

This was one of many turning points in Luther's life. To earn his doctorate, he would have to learn all the biblical languages and learn them well. And he would have to immerse himself into the Bible more comprehensively than he ever had. As Roland Bainton, perhaps Luther's best-known biographer, has written, "Anyone who seeks to discover the secret of Christianity is inevitably driven to the Bible, because Christianity is based on something which happened in the past, the incarnation of God in Christ at a definite point in history. The Bible records this event."[8]

So Luther was driven to the Bible, and it changed him. Now he spent his days fulfilling the daily disciplines of a monk but also studying—in the original languages and without the veneer of tradition—what Scripture actually said; not what the theologians and doctors of the Roman Church were teaching, but rather that which the pure Word of God revealed.

His knowledge of the biblical languages helped him see the many errors in the teaching of the church. While he discarded the fallacies of Rome, he also began to find help for his own soul.

Luther had long been haunted by the phrase "the justice of God." These words tormented him because he knew that if God was indeed a God of justice, then He would have no use for Martin Luther. Luther had failed, and he knew that God knew it. A just God would, therefore, be an angry God. A just God would be a God looking upon Martin Luther with wrath and only thoughts of judgment.

This was Luther's fearful mind-set for many years until he began to read the Bible in a pure and un-varnished way. Then the truth came to him. You may have heard that the revelation that set Luther free came to him as he was attempting to find relief from the intestinal trouble his frequent fasts gave him. It is true. Though the dawn of truth came progressively for Luther and not at one moment, his famous problem with constipation caused him to spend many hours seeking relief. During these hours he studied the Bible. So it is historically true that Martin Luther received revelation that led to his salvation while sitting in a pri-vate "closet." God does indeed have a sense of humor.

I'll let Luther tell you how God revealed the Scriptures to answer this question of God's justice.

> I greatly longed to understand Paul's Epistle to the Romans and nothing stood in the way but that one expression, "the justice of God," because I took it to mean that justice whereby God is just and deals justly in punishing the unjust....I stood before God as a sinner troubled in conscience, and I had no confidence that my

merit would assuage him. Therefore I did not love a just and angry God, but rather hated and murmured against him....

Night and day I pondered until I saw the connection between the justice of God and the statement that "the just shall live by his faith." Then I grasped that the justice of God is that righteousness by which through grace and sheer mercy God justifies us through faith. Thereupon I felt myself to be reborn and to have gone through open doors into paradise. The whole of Scripture took on a new meaning, and whereas before the "justice of God" had filled me with hate, now it became to me inexpressibly sweet in greater love. This passage of Paul became to me a gate to heaven.[9]

The great revelation had finally come to Luther. Men cannot earn their way to God's grace by works of the flesh. The justice of God could never be met by the natural efforts of mere men. God in His love made a way for His own justice to be answered: the sacrifice of Jesus Christ upon a cross! Now men are justified by believing in the work of heaven's crucified Lamb. In short, it is divine grace that connects man to God. It could never be by means of works or religious systems or a man harming himself to impress an angry deity. Grace is a gift, and it comes from a God who loves men and women more than the receivers of that matchless gift could possibly fully embrace or imagine.

Once these truths pierced Luther's soul, he was a man possessed by God. He was free from all the torment of so many years, and he was aflame with a simple truth: the just shall live by faith. Or as he began to speak of it to the many who followed him: *sola scriptura*—"only by scripture," *sola fide*—"only by faith," *sola gratia*—"only by grace."

There is so much more I would like to tell you about this man and how God used him to bring the message of grace to a world that had largely forgotten its gloriously freeing truth and reality. I will leave that for other authors and for other times. Yet I must rehearse that great action, that single day when history turned upon a single deed performed by a now-transformed Martin Luther. I must tell it because it is much the same kind of moment that we are desperate for and that I pray for today.

Picture the scene. Martin Luther is a busy professor and pastor who takes his calling to care for souls seriously. He is also a man newly born again and on fire with the great truth that the just shall live by faith. In what we have to see as divine timing, it is at this very moment that the medieval Roman Catholic Church initiates a practice that infuriates Luther and moves him to action. This practice was so corrupt that, thank God, the Catholic Church today condemns it.

There are two doctrines that collided to make the medieval church do such a foolish thing. First, the church taught the idea of purgatory. This was the belief that there was a kind of holding tank in eternity that was not heaven but not quite hell. Those who had died and had not been holy enough in this life to go to heaven were sent to purgatory, where they could be "purged" so they then would be qualified for heaven. I should hasten to say that this doctrine of purgatory was invented by men and is most certainly not taught in the Bible.

Nearly everyone in Luther's day believed in purgatory, but they also had begun to believe in another unbiblical idea that the medieval church was teaching. The church taught that some saints had lived such holy lives that they had excess goodness left over when they died. Not surprisingly, the church taught that the pope had control of this excess goodness and could dispense it to whomever he chose.

The pope in Luther's day was Leo X, and he was not the most principled man who ever held the office. He was busy trying to build what we know today as St. Peter's Basilica—the cathedral we think of as the heart of the Vatican in Rome—and Leo thought nothing of selling "indulgences" to raise money for St. Peter's.

These indulgences were like stock certificates for bits of the excess goodness of the departed saints. And if you bought these indulgences, you could have them applied to your dead relative's account and in essence, pay them out of purgatory and into heaven.

I want you to think about what this meant. Let's say you have tragically lost your child to a sickness. You long for that child to be in heaven. Then comes a preacher—a salesman, really—who tells you that the pope will apply the excess goodness of the departed saints to your child so he can go to heaven from purgatory. He will only do this, though, if you will buy indulgences, the profits of which will pay to build the pope's palace in Rome. Take a moment to consider the spiritual and psychological pressure of believing this. How would you feel if you didn't have any money? What would you believe about God and His kingdom if you really believed your child or your mother or your spouse would suffer in eternity because you didn't have enough money to pay the pope? It was a belief system spawned of Satan and conceived in hell, and it was spreading throughout the land as preachers/salesmen went about selling these indulgences.

One of these marketers, by the name of Tetzel, began selling indulgences near Luther's home and to the people he was pastoring. You can imagine Luther's response. Here was a man who had just been set aflame by the doctrine of justification by faith, and into his backyard comes a man selling tickets to heaven for the right price.

Luther was incensed. He could see a showdown

coming between those who understood salvation by faith and those who were agents of a corrupt religious system that was not based on faith in God but on fear, false doctrine, and most of all, money. When he could stand it no longer, Luther put his challenges to the corruption of the Church of his day into ninety-five statements—or as they are commonly referred to, Ninety-Five Theses—and made them public in the standard way for such things: he nailed them to the cathedral (church) door.

So on October 31 of 1517, inspired by holy indignation, Martin Luther posted his Ninety-Five Theses on the Wittenberg Church door and sparked a revolution. It was time, he said, to return to the pure gospel. It was time to return to the Bible. What people knew as the Christian church was in fact filled with corruption and needed reforming. Let it begin with these three simple truths: *sola scriptura, sola fide, sola gratia.*

I want you to feel this. Imagine that you have spent your whole life crawling on your knees before statues to win the approval of God. You have gone to church your whole life, but your priest doesn't consider you holy enough to touch or read a Bible. You have attended services all your days and have never been allowed to sing a hymn. You have only heard professional choirs do it. You are simply not holy enough. Imagine that you are encouraged by your ministers to believe that you are too filthy and unworthy to even approach God and that the closest to His presence you will ever get is talking to a priest behind a door with a sliding window.

Think about how you would react if this has been your whole life, and then Martin Luther appears, seemingly from nowhere, and announces that nothing you have been taught to believe and practice your entire life is true. None of it comes from the life or teaching of Jesus. None of it is biblical. You've been lied to. You've been deceived. You've been used. That system of works you've been required to practice for all those years? It's a lie. The truth is, you are accepted by God because Jesus Christ on Calvary's rail cleansed you. Live by faith. Live free. Divine grace reigns!

We cannot imagine the relief, the anger, and the joy people felt when they discovered this fundamental Bible truth. It shook the world—it changed the world! It transformed nations and entire systems of government. Education, the arts, and philosophy were irreversibly altered for all time and everywhere on the earth. This was not just an errant priest publishing a curious new doctrine that would soon fade into obscurity. This was a shift in the alignment of the church world—back to an emphasis on an individual's faith in a personal God who loved them passionately.

It was also a rediscovery that every believer is a priest to God, and every believer is called to use his or her gifts to serve God in this world. What became known as the Reformation may seem ordinary enough to us, but in those days it was so radical that it sent shock waves through every stratum of society.

I've recounted a very brief portion of Martin Luther's biography and legacy here because I believe we are living on the brink—on the edge, on the verge, on the precipice—of a third great awakening, a new reformation. I've declared it because we desperately need a reformation from two extremes that are concealing the gospel from men just as surely as the excesses of the medieval church did. First, there is the excess of a false version of grace that allows sin and carnality to rule and ruin lives. Second, there is the excess of humanly devised religious rules that have nothing to do with the law of God and that conceal the gospel by their harshness and domination.

We need a reformation of the church so that both of these extremes are eradicated—and we need it now.

I can do no better in closing this chapter than to include some of the words from Martin Luther's great hymn "A Mighty Fortress Is Our God." (I am convinced that just as much as in Luther's day, there is much in modern church music that needs a reformation as well.) This hymn captures much of the fire of the Reformation, and it gives us a holy vision of courage in proclaiming the great gospel of salvation by faith in Jesus Christ. Let it stir you, and let it inspire you to live even more passionately by faith.

A mighty fortress is our God, a bulwark never
    failing;
Our helper He, amid the flood of mortal ills
    prevailing:
For still our ancient foe doth seek to work us woe;
His craft and power are great, and, armed with
    cruel hate,
On earth is not his equal.
Did we in our own strength confide, our striving
    would be losing;
Were not the right Man on our side, the Man of
    God's own choosing:
Dost ask who that may be? Christ Jesus, it is He;
Lord Sabaoth, His Name, from age to age the
    same,
And He must win the battle.
And though this world, with devils filled, should
    threaten to undo us,
We will not fear, for God hath willed His truth to
    triumph through us:
The Prince of Darkness grim, we tremble not for
    him;
His rage we can endure, for lo, his doom is sure,
One little word shall fell him.
That word above all earthly powers, no thanks to
    them, abideth;
The Spirit and the gifts are ours through Him
    who with us sideth:
Let goods and kindred go, this mortal life also;
The body they may kill: God's truth abideth still,
His kingdom is forever.[10]

# CHAPTER 4

# What Seems Good to the Holy Spirit

*If we give God service it must be because He gives us grace. We work for Him because He works in us.*

—CHARLES H. SPURGEON

O NE OF THE things I love about the Bible is its grit. (I may not be witty, but you can't argue, I'm gritty.) It tells a story straight and does not exclude all the grime and the muck of the human condition. God doesn't hide the tough stuff from us. In fact, He wants us to learn from the darkness and the light, from mankind at its best as well as from mankind at its most heinous and vile.

As opposed to the carefully contrived situations on so-called reality shows today, there is real drama in the Bible when we view it this way. Nowhere is this more so than in the story of the council of Jerusalem we find in the Book of Acts. I think we miss the importance of this moment in early Christian history. We miss the great clash of visions in this episode, and so we do not realize how perilously close the early church came to missing its great mission of reaching the world with the gospel of Christ. At the heart of the issue was the question of law and grace, which is the very question we are exploring in this book. Let's look at the great saga of the council of Jerusalem as we find it in Acts 15.

This gathering took place in about AD 45, which means it occurred just fifteen years after the crucifixion and resurrection of Jesus. The gospel had been spreading for a decade and a half by then, and it had moved beyond the Jewish world to the wider world of the Gentiles. This is what prompted the great crisis that the council of Jerusalem had to solve.

As the Book of Acts chronicles the spread of the gospel, it naturally follows the travels and transitions of Paul. His story is all about this matter of law and grace and how the gospel should be lived among the Gentiles.

After Paul became a believer and was reconciled to the fledgling Christian church, he spent time under the tutelage of Barnabas and began preaching in places like Damascus and Jerusalem. Unlike much modern preaching, which is calculated to keep everyone happy, Paul's preaching was so bold and innovative that it caused riots. The church leaders finally had to send him back to his hometown of Tarsus for his own safety.

Our story really begins when we read the opening lines of Acts 13. They describe how at the city of Antioch there was a gathering of prophets and teachers. Paul was among them. Everyone was fasting and ministering to the Lord when the Holy Spirit spoke and said that the leaders should commission Paul and Barnabas for the work to which God had called them. The leaders obeyed. They spent additional time in fasting and prayer and then laid hands on Paul and Barnabas before sending them off on what we know as the first missionary journey.

Now these two men did exactly what we would expect two Hebrew Christians to do: they went about ministering in synagogues. Their ministry was mainly one of telling their fellow Jews that the Messiah had come. They ministered first in a synagogue on the island of Cyprus, and then at a synagogue in a region called Pisidia, which is roughly where south-central Turkey is today. God did great things through Paul and Barnabas. In fact, God performed such amazing signs and wonders at their hands that the Jews in Pisidia became jealous of the huge crowds the two men attracted. Soon the Jewish leaders began opposing them. They turned some of the leading citizens of the city against the apostles, and they heaped abuse on them publicly.

This infuriated Paul, who turned to those who came against them and said, "It was necessary that the word of God should be spoken to you first. But seeing you reject it, and judge yourselves unworthy of eternal life, we are turning to the Gentiles. For thus has the Lord commanded us: 'I have established you to be a light of the Gentiles, that you may bring salvation to the ends of the earth.'"[1]

So Paul and Barnabas began preaching the gospel among the Gentiles. They were among the first Christian leaders to see that the Gentiles could be saved just like the Jews, and that God was reaching out to the Gentiles in love and in power. When the two missionaries returned to their home church and reported what had been happening among the Gentiles, the believers rejoiced. They recognized that Old Testament prophecy was being fulfilled: God was empowering His young church to be a light to the Gentiles.

This is when an unforeseen controversy broke out. There is almost always controversy when God is doing something new and when news of a pioneering work reaches the ears of those who have no pioneering spirit. This has been true throughout history, and it was certainly true in the first-century church as well.

As we start reading at the beginning of Acts 15, we find that some of the Jewish Christians in Jerusalem were upset that the Gentiles were being allowed to believe in Jesus and join the Christian church without first having to submit to Jewish standards and practices. These Jewish Christians were teaching that "unless you are circumcised in the tradition of Moses, you cannot be saved."[2] In other words, according to them, the Gentiles had to become Jews before they could become Christians. Obedience to the law had to precede faith. This was what many in Jerusalem had begun to believe.

It's easy for us all these years later to be irritated with these early Jewish Christians. It sounds as though all they wanted to do was put people in bondage and keep the Gentiles out of the kingdom of God. It goes deeper than that though, and we don't catch the drama of the whole affair unless we take what these Hebrew Christians were saying seriously.

We have to understand how a committed Jew at the time of Jesus would have perceived a Gentile. For a man of the covenant—a man deeply devoted to pleasing the God of Abraham, Isaac, and Jacob—a Gentile lived an astonishingly filthy and immoral life. I'll need to be very graphic for a moment to help you understand why this was so.

It wasn't just that Gentiles ate pork, didn't keep the Sabbath, or didn't read and memorize the law of God. These things were true, but these weren't what gave such offense to the Jews. It was far deeper than that. When a Jew at the time of Jesus looked out on the Roman world, he saw indescribable immorality, idolatry, blasphemy, and perversion. Men were worshipped as gods. Pagan temples were little more than houses of prostitution in which "worshippers" would have sexual intercourse with "priestesses." Inconvenient newborn babies were routinely left to die of exposure on the city walls or drowned in nearby streams. The elderly, the infirm, and those who had committed some act of betrayal were expected to commit suicide so they would not burden or dishonor society. Orgies were commonplace. The most shocking perversions were offered as entertainment. Drunkenness and gluttony were in fashion, and let's not forget that human beings were slaughtered for entertainment in the coliseums of the Roman Empire.

You can see, then, that a Jew in Jesus' day did not just look out upon the Roman world and see people of a different religion or culture. He looked upon the Roman world and saw Satan and his hordes in complete control of men's lives.

So what happened when a Jew at that time became a Christian? In the early days the new Christian movement was comprised entirely of Jewish believers. There were no questions among them about matters of cleanliness or purity. Everyone agreed, without even discussing it, upon the standards written in the law of God.

Then this fellow Paul began reporting that the Gentiles were being saved and coming into the church. You can imagine what a Jew would think. "What? The devil worshippers? The idolaters? The shedders of blood? Those who have lent their bodies to the most filthy practices? Those people are being saved? Well, thank God for His mercy to the Gentiles. We want them to be converted, but they will have to get pure by obeying the law first. We can't have their wicked ways coming into the church unchallenged."

This was the issue for the early church in AD 45: How should the Gentiles be saved? How could the great unwashed become clean enough for salvation?

I suppose that, like me, you are stunned to see that

the Pharisees were part of the problem. The Pharisees? In the church? You would think that the Pharisees would either have run from the gospel message or would have stopped being Pharisees once they became Christians. After all, these were the people who were proud of their strict obedience to the law, who did everything they could to separate themselves from ordinary people, and who opposed Jesus at every opportunity. Jesus reserved some of His most withering criticisms for the Pharisees. But no: right there in verse 5 of Acts 15 we see that "some believers of the sect of the Pharisees rose up, saying, 'It is necessary to circumcise them, and to command them to keep the Law of Moses.'"

Oh no—not the Pharisees again! They did everything they could to cause trouble for Jesus all His days on earth, and here they are troubling the Christian church—and from within. It says there were believers who were Pharisees. You would have thought that old Pharisee spirit would have been cast out the minute any of them accepted Jesus as their Savior and Messiah.

So the early church was in crisis and had to call a meeting of the leaders to work this thing out. Over several days of meeting in Jerusalem, the Christian Pharisees made their case, and then Peter, Paul, and Barnabas spoke movingly about what God had revealed to them and how the gospel had spread among the Gentiles. Keep in mind that this council was conducted among those who were accustomed to debate and dispute. It did not resemble a sleepy town hall meeting. Voices were raised. Discussion was heated. Passions were evident.

Try to feel this as well as think this. It was a moment that would change everything one way or the other. If the church decided that the Gentiles had to become Jews to become Christians, it would mean they would have to navigate high walls and narrow gates to get into the kingdom of God. It would also mean that the church would always be Jewish in character. Yet if the church decided that the Gentiles did not have to observe the Jewish law to become Christians, it would mean both that a great harvest among the Gentiles awaited, but also that the church would cease to be Jewish and would probably cease to be based in Jerusalem.

It was the greatest crisis the young church had faced, and it would determine the nature of Christianity for the rest of history. Fortunately, the Holy Spirit spoke. And fortunately, the early church listened.

It was the apostle James, the Lord's brother, who led this gathering, and we should always be thankful for his wisdom and insight. When all had been heard, he stood and addressed the council. He said that what Paul and Barnabas had described of God's work among the Gentiles was in keeping with the prophecies of Scripture. He said that nothing should be done to make it difficult for the Gentiles to turn to God. The church should not require the Gentiles to become Jews first and submit to the law. However, he was mindful of the difficulties that Jews and Gentiles worshipping in the same congregations presented, and so he gave some commonsense guidelines that the Gentile believers should observe that would prevent unnecessary conflict with Jewish believers. Among these were that they abstain from food polluted by idols, that they avoid sexual immorality, and that they not eat meat that was raw or improperly bled. Otherwise, let them come to Jesus by faith like all of us Hebrew Christians.

The elders asked their Gentile brethren to observe these guidelines not because their salvation depended on it, but because, as James said, "'They should do these things, because for a long time in every city the law of Moses has been taught [Moses has been preached/proclaimed; referring to the Torah (the Law)]. And it is still read in the synagogue every Sabbath day.' [These guidelines were to keep from offending pious Jews in the community and so promote unity in the Church.]"[3]

In a sweet letter the council sent out to the Gentile churches, the elders said that they were sorry the Gentile believers had been troubled by this controversy. Men would be sent to convey the council's ruling. It had "seemed good to the Holy Spirit" that the elders not place any burden upon their fellow believers that would keep them from accepting Jesus as Savior, or make their walk of faith more difficult. The elders did ask that they observe certain restrictions that would enable them to avoid conflict with Jewish believers who were still careful to obey the prescriptions of the law, especially regarding meat offered to idols. And welcome to the family of God.

This ruling by the leaders of the early church was genius. It is a guide to us today. It established in AD 45 what Martin Luther had to reestablish 1,500 years later: "the just shall live by faith." However, the elders also recognized that while our relationship with God does not depend on a set of written ordinances, the law of God does contain guidelines and principles that are both universal and beneficial. However, any effort to try to fulfill the requirements of God's law according to our own strength is doomed to failure. Martin Luther discovered this. I did as well. You probably did too.

As New Testament believers, we do not obey the law of God because someone says we must. We meet and even exceed the law's requirements because of the love of God that was implanted in our hearts when we received Jesus as Savior. Look at it this way. No Christian husband loves his wife because a written law says he should. He loves his wife because his heart is filled with love for her. He's not coerced to love her— he loves her because he can't help it. Love overflows out of his heart toward the woman that he made a covenant commitment to love and cherish for the rest of his days. He's not going to avoid adultery because there is a written law that says he should. He wouldn't think of coveting someone else's wife, because he loves his own wife as Christ loves the church.

Paul said, "Love does no wrong to one's neighbor [it never hurts anybody]. Therefore love meets all the requirements *and* is the fulfilling of the Law."[4] Jesus gave us important insight when answering this question: "'Sir, which is the most important command in the laws of Moses?' Jesus replied, '"Love the Lord your God with all your heart, soul, and mind." This is the first and greatest commandment. The second most important is similar: "Love your neighbor as much as you love yourself." All the other commandments and all the demands of the prophets stem from these two laws and are fulfilled if you obey them. Keep only these and you will find that you are obeying all the others.'"[5]

When the elders of the early church gave these guidelines to Gentile believers, they did so from a practical perspective, not because they wanted to lay a burden on them that was impractical or impossible. Their expectation was that Gentile Christians would express the love of God toward their Jewish fellow believers by avoiding the practices that were the most likely to offend them. These were not the demands of a law that was impossible to keep, but directions that appealed to the love of God that compelled them to comply. Love, not the law, was the expectation of the church and its leaders.

We see then that grace rules our lives, but grace is not without a need for boundaries, guidelines for behavior and ethical demands. Grace sets me free from the bondage of the law, but since it is the law of God we are dealing with, there is wisdom and truth to be found in it.

Did the apostles put the early church under the law? Absolutely not. They understood that believers are freed from attempting to comply with the law's demands and are accepted by God only through faith in the finished work of Jesus. Yet the early church leaders also understood that the law does reveal what pleases God. It gives principles that guide Christian conduct so that God is honored, boundaries of holiness are maintained, and the Holy Spirit can change hearts.

The early church set us on a course we desperately need to reclaim today. Grace is not the absence of ethics or boundaries or principles of conduct or truth to guide our steps. Grace—uncovered, unfiltered, undeserved—is freeing us from believing that any of these save us. Grace is understanding that only Jesus could live up to God's law and that through faith in Him the righteous demands of a holy God are fulfilled. But grace is not the abolition of all standards, all truths that guide conduct, or all boundaries that define and distinguish between the holy and the profane.

The wisdom of the early church should become our wisdom. "Jesus has set us free," they proclaim, "but Jesus has set us free to live in whatever way pleases God. This way of living is not our salvation. Jesus accomplished that. This way of living is our grateful response to what we have received."

This was the wisdom of the council of Jerusalem in AD 45, and it is truth that we must recover today. Law and grace work together. Both are from God and were meant for our good. Both now must be woven into our lives in the tapestry of faith to which God has called us.

The tremendous freedom God has given us is greater than any of us can imagine. We are certainly delivered from the bondage and condemnation of attempting to live up to the requirements of a law we can never fulfill, since we know that Jesus has fulfilled the law for us. Yet we also have the liberty of wise boundaries defined in that law so that we do not have the burden of deciding right and wrong for ourselves. And on some matters God even allows us to follow our own conscience so that each person can choose what is best for himself or herself. There could be no greater safety and no greater joy than we find in the freedom God has given us in Christ.

We must protect this precious gift and not allow

a slow slide into bondage through either extremes of grace or extremes of law. Now is the time for the wisdom of our fathers of faith, the great love of God, and the freedom we have in Christ to prevail.

# PART II

# PRINCIPLES

T IS TRUE that Christians are freed from the rule of law. Yet it is also true that the law is a revelation of God's character and God's will. How can we discern this revelation? How can we take from the absolutes of God the wisdom we need for living and yet avoid the temptation to make those absolutes into a legalistic system of salvation? This is the heart of a biblical approach to this matter of law and grace. So in the chapters that follow, I want to share how we can unearth the principles for Christian living that come from Scripture and the work of the Holy Spirit in our hearts. I want to show you how to walk that glorious highway of holiness that God summons His people to walk. Here you will find the great adventure of living a life of both law and grace.

# CHAPTER 5

# The Law and the Cross

*They who truly come to God for mercy,*
*come as beggars, and not as creditors:*
*they come for mere mercy, for sovereign*
*grace, and not for anything that is due.*

—JONATHAN EDWARDS

L ET ME SHARE with you a truth about law and grace that we seem to have forgotten—one that our fathers knew but our churches no longer teach, and that we are poorer for living without. To realize how law and grace should shape us today, we have to understand what the law was before grace came to us in Jesus Christ, and then we have to know what the law is now that we are under grace.

When we look back upon the law as we find it in the Old Testament, we can easily see that there were two kinds of law. Not two laws—just two parts of the same law. There was the ceremonial law, and there was the civil law.

The ceremonial law is fairly easy to identify. This part of the law related to all the ceremonies, the rituals, the feasts, and the sacrifices required of the people under the Old Covenant. This was the law that governed who could be priests, what they should wear, how they should make sacrifices, and how they should advise the people. This same ceremonial law prescribed the exact way every sacrifice was to be made. It set the Hebrew calendar in place, with all its feasts and holy days and observances. This law also laid out in great detail the precise blueprint for the tabernacle—every pole, every animal skin used in it, every utensil of worship, and every piece of furniture—and all the regulations that pertained to it.

Every ceremony required of the people of God under the Old Covenant—from the circumcision of a child on the eighth day to the specifications of the great Day of Atonement—was defined under the ceremonial law of God. Put another way, it was the liturgical law or the law of religious rituals.

Now, what we know about this ceremonial law is that it was all fulfilled in the life and ministry of Jesus Christ. This is the good news of the gospel. All the ceremonies required in the Old Testament pointed to Jesus and were fulfilled by Him. In fact, in a very real sense, much of what we call Christianity is the Old Testament fulfilled.

Consider:

- The Old Covenant requires a high priest. The New Covenant gives us Jesus as the High Priest.

- The Old Covenant gives us a tabernacle. The New Covenant gives us heaven, or a heavenly tabernacle.

- The Old Covenant gives us the sacrifice of animals and the shedding of their blood for atonement for sin. The New Covenant gives us the once-and-for-all sacrifice of Jesus Christ and the shedding of His blood as our atonement for sin.

- The Old Covenant gives us numerous sacrifices and offerings. The New Covenant gives us a lifestyle of generosity and worship.

- The Old Covenant gives us holy days. The New Covenant declares that every day is holy to the Lord.

- The Old Covenant gives us the nation of Israel as the people of God. The New Covenant gives us "one new man"—a combination of Jews and Gentiles who believe in Jesus Christ as Savior—and a commission to take the gospel to every people on earth.

Every part of the ceremonial law of the Old Covenant pointed to Jesus and was fulfilled by Jesus. In other words, when the Old Testament ceremonial law passed through the cross, it was completed once and for all. For followers of Christ there are no more animal sacrifices to be made. Every believer is now a priest unto God and recognizes one great High Priest. All believers worship in a heavenly tabernacle, before a heavenly altar, and offer the fruit of their lips as offerings to God in worship.

The Bible makes this very clear in the following few verses.

> Therefore let no one judge you regarding food, or drink, or in respect of a holy day or new moon or sabbath days. These are shadows of things to come, but the substance belongs to Christ.[1]

> For the law is a shadow of the good things to come, and not the very image of those things. It could never by the same sacrifices, which they offer continually year after year, perfect those who draw near. Otherwise, would they not have ceased to be offered, since the worshippers, once purified, would no longer be conscious of sins?[2]

> If perfection were attained through the Levitical priesthood (for through it the people received the law), what further need was there that another priest should rise in the order of Melchizedek, rather than established in the order of Aaron? For a change in the priesthood necessitates a change in the law.[3]

So you see that the ceremonial law is fulfilled in Jesus Christ. Though it teaches us and helps us understand what our Savior did for us, it is passed away—fulfilled—completed—made new. This is the great truth at the heart of our Christian faith. All that

God instituted among the Jews of the Old Covenant explains what Jesus has done for us.

The ceremonial law is fulfilled. However, the civil law—what some call the moral law—was there too. This civil or moral law was God's will for the way men treated one another, the condition of their hearts toward God, His commandments for the running of a society, and His will in a thousand practical matters. This part of the law governed everything from lawsuits to prisons, from marriage to honor for parents, from treatment of the poor to the treatment of strangers in the land. None of this was merely ceremonial. It was the way God wanted things to be in a society and among a people who wished to please Him.

To get a better understanding of this kind of law, we can begin with the Ten Commandments. Though I hope you have these famous commandments memorized, take a long, slow look at them again. They are recorded in your Bible in Exodus 20:3–17 and again in Deuteronomy 5:7–21.

> You shall have no other gods before Me.
>
> You shall not make for yourself any graven idol, or any likeness of anything that is in heaven above, or that is in the earth beneath, or that is in the water below the earth. You shall not bow down to them or serve them....
>
> You shall not take the name of the LORD your

God in vain, for the LORD will not hold guiltless anyone who takes His name in vain.

Remember the Sabbath day and keep it holy.…

Honor your father and your mother, that your days may be long in the land which the LORD your God is giving you.

You shall not murder.

You shall not commit adultery.

You shall not steal.

You shall not bear false witness against your neighbor.

You shall not covet your neighbor's house; you shall not covet your neighbor's wife, or his manservant, or his maidservant, or his ox, or his donkey, or anything that is your neighbor's.

With the possible exception of commandment number four, none of these commandments were purely for the Old Covenant people or were changed in any way by what Jesus did for us on the cross.[4] If anything, Jesus actually strengthened and internalized some of these commandments. Remember His famous statement in Matthew 5:17–18? "Do not think that I have come to abolish the Law or the Prophets. I have not come to abolish, but to fulfill. For truly I say to you, until heaven and earth pass away, not one dot or one mark will pass from the law until all be fulfilled."

We should put these words of Jesus up against another statement He made: "You have heard that it was said by the ancients, 'You shall not commit adultery.' But I say to you that whoever looks on a woman to lust after her has committed adultery with her already in his heart."[5]

What we see in all of this is that while the ceremonial law has been fulfilled, the civil or moral law still gives us both absolutes and wisdom for living. Take a look at just a few of the great principles of God that are found in this civil or moral law. In His great civil law God gives us commandments and guidelines that do the following:

- Forbid kidnapping

- Forbid sex outside of marriage

- Forbid prostitution

- Forbid adultery

- Regulate divorce

- Define who may marry whom

- Set boundaries for waging war

- Establish how a court should hear evidence

- Establish guidelines for lending

- Provide for the protection of private property

- Provide for the care of the poor

- Define responsibility for personal injury

- Provide for protection of women and orphans

- Forbid deceptive business practices

- Establish guidelines for promises and contracts

- Regulate the treatment of servants and employees

- Forbid theft

- Forbid murder

- Forbid lying and giving false testimony before a court

- Forbid covetousness

- Establish cleanliness laws for diseases and bloody injuries

- Forbid bestiality

- Forbid disobedience to parents

- Forbid rape

- Forbid witchcraft

The law of God relates to far more topics than these, but let's stop here. I think it is fair to say that nearly all Christians throughout all the history of the church would agree that the laws listed above should continue to carry authority for believers. In other words, nothing about these laws changed after Jesus died on the cross. Adultery, theft, lying, and covetousness are just as wrong today as they were thousands of years ago. They are not symbolic or ceremonial laws that Jesus fulfilled. The instructions God gave regarding all of these areas are not all specifically mentioned in the Ten Commandments, but they are all based upon them and are not just suggestions. Without some form of moral law, humans would never be able to live at peace with one another and would quickly destroy themselves. The conditions that existed before the flood of Noah's day testify to this with great clarity.

Christians have had to figure out how to apply some of these laws, of course. While we do believe that children should obey their parents, we don't stone disobedient children these days, as it says to do in Deuteronomy 21:18–21. We should all be glad about that! Yet a bit of uncertainty about the application doesn't remove the truth of the principle—children should obey their parents.

The important point here is that while the ceremonial law of God has been fulfilled in the life, death, and resurrection of Jesus, the moral or civil law has not been ended or abolished. In fact, as we've seen, Jesus actually strengthened a few of the laws He mentioned. A man should not only abstain from adultery, Jesus said that man should also refrain from lusting in his heart. Jesus made this requirement bigger, bolder, and deeper. He didn't say it no longer applied to those who received His grace.

I've taken all this time and space to distinguish the ceremonial law from the civil or moral law because I believe it establishes the all-important point that I'm trying to make in these pages: there are absolutes from God that we should know and obey. Read this last sentence again. *There are absolutes from God that we should know and obey.* This means that the grace of God and the law of God are meant to work together in the life of a Christian. It means that God's grace and God's requirements go hand in hand.

Now, let me shout this next point loud and often. We do not heed God's absolutes to earn salvation. Never! We can do nothing to earn our salvation. It is the gift of God. We are saved by grace. We are saved because of what Jesus did for us on the cross. Salvation is a free gift, and no man can earn it.

These principles of the law that I mention above are important to us because once we have received God's awesome grace, we should be so passionately in love with Him that we want to please Him. We want to align our lives with His will. We want to do whatever honors Him. We obey out of gratitude. We heed not because we always understand the reasons behind God's requirements, but because we understand that He is good and He would never require anything of us that is not for our benefit. We align ourselves so our lives are consistent with the One who bought us and pleasing to the One to whom we owe everything.

This is much like what happens when a man marries a woman. He marries her because he loves her. He can't imagine his life without her. So he asks her to marry him, and she says yes. He's dumbfounded. This gorgeous, amazing creature has agreed to be his wife. What a miracle. Then, once he starts living with her, he wants to please her. He's so in love, so grateful. So he pays attention to what she likes, what makes her happy. He also pays attention to what displeases her. It turns out she doesn't like it when he balls up his gym socks and plays trash can basketball all through the house. Before he got married, his buddies thought this was hilarious. She doesn't. He stops. Why? Because she laid down the law? No, because he loves her and wants to please her.

He also finds out that she likes to have the bed turned down for her at night. He starts doing that for her. Why? Because he's her slave? No, he's her husband, and he wants to see her happy. So each evening he removes the score of little pillows ladies manage to put on a bed and turns the covers down for her. It pleases him because it pleases her. It's his delight. He loves her so much and loves loving her.

That's how it is with those of us who believe. We are so grateful that God has extended His grace and favor to us, we would do anything for Him. So when He says that it pleases Him for us to be generous to the poor, or to keep lust out of our hearts, or to care for those who have hurt themselves on our property, or to not get drunk, or to welcome the stranger in the land, or to obey our parents, or to avoid the divorce that God hates—we do it. It pleases our Lord and Savior.

This is what it means for law and grace to go hand in hand. And the glorious good news is that God is so gracious, He does not leave us to obey His precepts in our own power. He gives us the power to do His will. Philippians 2:13 says, "For it is [not your strength, but it is] God who is effectively at work in you, both to will and to work [that is, strengthening, energizing, and creating in you the longing and the ability to fulfill your purpose] for His good pleasure" (AMP).

What a Father!

What a God!

What a joy to do His will!

# CHAPTER 6

# The Heart of the Matter

*I have never met a person I could
despair of, or lose all hope for,
after discerning what lies in me
apart from the grace of God.*

—OSWALD CHAMBERS

W E LEARNED AN important truth in the last chapter. I want to make sure we don't let it slip from our minds. The law of God, though it could not save us because we could not live up to it, nevertheless reveals God and much of His will. That law is holy and it is pure. The ceremonial part of that law anticipated Jesus, His sacrifice, and His high priestly ministry at the right hand of God. Most of us wouldn't have known what a high priest or a sacrifice or a tabernacle was if it hadn't been for the law. Because the law has come to us through the Scriptures, we understand not only the Father's great holiness, but also the power of what Jesus did for us and still does for us now in heaven.

We also learned that while the ceremonial law is fulfilled, the civil or moral law continues to give us revelation of God's will. We know not to murder, not to steal, not to lie, and not to mistreat strangers—along with a thousand other precepts—because we have a revelation of God's will through His precious law.

I should say it once again: we are not saved by obedience to this law. We are saved by the redemption Jesus purchased for us on the cross and by our faith in that sacrifice. The law remains in our lives as a revelation of

God's will, though, as a guide to what pleases God and to what is best for our lives in this world.

It is here that we must be careful. As you've read in my own story and as you may know from your own experience, we Christians can create legalistic systems even out of the grace-tempered law we have on this new covenant side of the cross. We've proven that we can receive the liberating grace of God and then foolishly take the principles that should guide us and make them into a new form of bondage—a whole new system of legalism that then breeds fear, oppression, and strife.

We are missing the matter of the heart when we do this. We are missing the truth that is at the core of the gospel, and it is that Jesus comes not just to save us but also to remake us in His image. The reality is that grace tempered by law shows us what we should be, while the Spirit of God refashions us so that we can be all that we should be. And all this leads us to the purpose we are destined for: to be like Jesus.

Let's begin with that powerful statement Paul gives us in his Magna Carta of faith, the Book of Romans. He wrote, "For those God foreknew he also predestined to be conformed to the image of his Son, that he might be the firstborn among many brothers and sisters."[1] There it is. There is the vision that should enflame every Christian heart. We are destined to be conformed to the image of Jesus. Our purpose, and thus our passion, is to be remade to be like Him.

This is where the whole matter of law and grace converges. Some want complete freedom to indulge themselves, and they call it grace. Others want binding precepts for every situation, and they want them ironclad. Most believers are arrayed somewhere between these two. Yet once we understand that we are intended for conformity to the image of Jesus, all extremes, all excuses, all schemes to indulge ourselves in the name of faith *and* all clinging to the laws of men dissolve in the simple truth that both law and grace serve the purpose of making us into the image of Jesus Christ.

In short, extremes of law and grace fail to reach the heart of the matter, which is the heart of God transplanted into us.

I have always loved that portion of the Book of Jeremiah in which God gives us a glimpse of the people He longs for. This was recorded while the people of God were in Babylonian captivity, long before they were given leave to return to their own land. God, speaking through His prophet, uses that moment to look through the telescope of time and describe the kind of covenant and the kind of people that will be a delight to Him. It is a beautiful passage of Scripture, and it is also the only place in the Old Testament in which the phrase *new covenant* is used.

> Surely, the days are coming, says the Lord, when
> I will make a new covenant with the house of
> Israel and with the house of Judah. It will not be

according to the covenant that I made with their fathers in the day that I took them by the hand to bring them out of the land of Egypt, because they broke My covenant, although I was a husband to them, says the LORD. But this shall be the covenant that I will make with the house of Israel after those days, says the LORD: I will put My law within them and write it in their hearts; and I will be their God, and they shall be My people. They shall teach no more every man his neighbor and every man his brother, saying, "Know the LORD," for they all shall know Me, from the least of them to the greatest of them, says the LORD, for I will forgive their iniquity, and I will remember their sin no more.[2]

What moves me about this grand passage is how God describes the new covenant. It will be a covenant in which the law is written on the heart. In the first covenant, God gave the law and people were required to obey it. The focus seemed to be on externals—on the doing and the observing. Yet in the new covenant the emphasis shifts to the heart. This doesn't diminish the absolutes of God in any way, but it does make the source of the obedience to God's will a matter of heart rather than a matter of external duties alone.

I think we can glimpse what God wants here. He desires a people who have absorbed His law into their inner being. He intends to have a people who embody the law and don't just observe it as a matter of obligation. The law of God lives in them, delights them, comprises their meditation, and makes them into a people given to God.

In fact, one of the things that so moves me about this passage is how in one sentence God says He will "put My law within them and write it in their hearts" and in the very next sentence He says that "I will be their God, and they shall be My people." There is an unmistakable emphasis on heart and relationship here. God is clearly saying that the people of the new covenant will be a people whose hearts and minds are filled with the revelation of God through His law, and that this will be part of a living relationship with Him.

How beautifully this expresses what God desires from His New Testament, new covenant people. He doesn't want a lawless people. He also doesn't want a people of law apart from relationship. What He is looking for is a people who love His law—the revelation of God through His statutes and precepts—and who live in a dynamic relationship with Him.

Once we glimpse this vision of God's law in our hearts, we can begin to understand the glory of Psalm 119. This is the longest psalm in the entire Book of Psalms, and it is completely devoted to delighting in the law of the Lord. It would be easy for a Christian to look upon this and think it is just an Old Testament sentiment for an Old Testament people who haven't been touched by grace. But that's not what we should conclude once we've read the words from Jeremiah I've cited above. Once we have this "law and relationship" vision in our hearts, we can enter into the psalmist's delight in the law of the Lord. Listen to how law and relationship blend in this great poem of devotion.

> Let Your mercies come to me, O LORD, even Your deliverance according to Your word. So I shall have an answer for him who reproaches me, for I trust in Your word. Do not take the word of truth out of my mouth, for I have hoped in Your judgments. So I shall keep Your law continually, forever and ever. I will walk in an open space, for I seek Your precepts. I will speak of Your testimonies also before kings and will not be ashamed. I will delight in Your commandments, which I have loved. My hands I will lift up unto Your commandments, which I have loved; I will meditate on Your statutes.[3]

You see, this psalmist has found what a new covenant believer is supposed to find in the law of God. He has discovered that the law is a revelation of the God whom he loves. He has found that there is power and life in the law of God. The psalmist meditates upon the law and celebrates the law. He loves the law, because it reveals God. It shows the way of God. The law of the Lord has become his delight. This was as close as he could come to the kind of intimate, personal relationship a new covenant believer has with God.

There is also power in this law, these words of the living God. In verse 11 of this great psalm, the writer proclaims, "Your word I have hidden in my heart, that I might not sin against You."[4] He has found the power of the law/word of God to change the human heart.

The focus is upon the heart. This is what God was longing for when He spoke those powerful words through the prophet Jeremiah. It was as though He was saying, "I am weary of a people who reject Me as their lover and their husband. I am looking forward to My new covenant people. I'm looking for those who will welcome My laws and truths into their hearts and minds and who will live in relationship with Me. These I will forgive. These will know Me. These will be close to My heart."

Yet this matter of walking close to God's heart requires something additional. It requires that we open our lives to the Spirit of God. The Spirit is sent to live in us to remake us according to the will of God. We find this theme in another of the great passages of the Old Testament. In the Book of Ezekiel, we come to a passage in which God is again describing the unfaithfulness of Israel. As He did through the prophet Jeremiah, God looks down the corridors of time and describes what He is going to do to the people of Israel in order to make them a people after His own heart.

> Also, I will give you a new heart, and a new spirit I will put within you. And I will take away the stony heart out of your flesh, and I will give you a heart of flesh. I will put My Spirit within you and cause you to walk in My statutes, and you will keep My judgments and do them. You will dwell in the land that I gave to your fathers. And you will be My people, and I will be your God.[5]

You see the all-important emphasis here. God does not give us His Spirit to free us from moral absolutes. He gives us His Spirit so we are transformed to the point that we can fulfill His moral absolutes. We yearn to do His will. This is what those who advocate for a hyper-grace, liberty-at-all-costs perspective are misunderstanding. We are saved and filled with the Spirit so that we will be transformed into God's image. As that process unfolds, we are passionate to please the Father and to do His will. This means we delight in the law and decrees of God. We aren't saved and filled with the Spirit to pursue our own interests, our own passions, or our own pleasures.

These beautiful, poetic Old Testament passages feed perfectly into the truth we find in our New Testament. Just think of all the marvelous New Testament passages that speak of our hearts being transformed so we can do the will of the heavenly Father.

Therefore we conclude that a man is justified by faith without the works of the law....Do we then make the law void through faith? God forbid! Instead, we establish the law.[6]

For what the law could not do, in that it was weak through the flesh, God did by sending His own Son in the likeness of sinful flesh, and concerning sin, He condemned sin in the flesh, in order that the righteous requirement of the law might be fulfilled in us, who walk not according to the flesh but according to the Spirit.[7]

For those who live according to the flesh set their minds on the things of the flesh, but those who live according to the Spirit, the things of the Spirit. To be carnally minded is death, but to be spiritually minded is life and peace, for the carnal mind is hostile toward God, for it is not subject to the law of God, nor indeed can it be.[8]

Christ is the end of the law unto righteousness for every one who believes.[9]

Do you see the power of this? This is how great the salvation of God is for those who believe. They are empowered so they can do the will of God. Once they were under the law and fell short. Now they are under a law of faith by which they receive all that Jesus has provided by His obedience and sacrifice. They "fulfill the law" because they live their lives by faith in Jesus, who fulfilled all righteousness and then died with all our sinfulness upon Him. It means that the saved now are filled with the power to do the will of God, to please Him and live for His glory. This is the good news of the gospel of Jesus Christ.

What drains this good news of its power is when some believe salvation is an *escape* from God's standards and boundaries. It's a lie. Salvation is instead a *rescue* from sin and a remaking of our lives so we can fulfill God's standards and live within His boundaries. In other words, salvation allows us to fulfill the grace-tempered law of God. The curse of the law was not that the law was a curse. That's how many Christians speak of the law today. No, the curse of the law was that there was no grace to keep it. The law became a curse to the people of God because they constantly fell short of it, which meant it was nothing but condemnation to them. The good news is that grace has come through Jesus Christ, and that grace is the power of God that allows us to live according to God's standards.

It is this matter of the transformed heart that should quell all legalism and all license passing itself off as Christian liberty. If my heart is changed so that I want to fulfill the law of God, I don't need a system of legalism to force me toward righteousness. And if my heart is changed so I want to do the will of God, I also won't stray into realms of my own willfulness that are contrary to God's will. With my heart changed by the Spirit, I can walk the certain road of righteousness without falling into the ditch of legalism on the one side or the ditch of license on the other side.

You see, the law serves a purpose. It is our tutor, our teacher. Paul told the Galatians that "the law was our guardian until Christ came that we might be justified by faith. Now that this faith has come, we are no longer under a guardian."[10] Think of this word *guardian* as meaning something like a nanny or a tutor. When we were young, we needed the constant reminding and discipline of a parent or a tutor to teach us what was right. My father was skilled in keeping me in line when I was a child and needed that reinforcement. But when we become adults, hopefully we have so internalized the lessons of our youth that the discipline of nannies and tutors isn't necessary any longer. Their lessons have become part of us. Rather than obeying a restriction applied to us from the outside, we have an impulse to obey built into our innermost being. We obey because we want to, not because someone else tells us to.

This is just the way it is with the law of God. We needed the law to show us God and His will. Yet with the Spirit, we don't need that external reinforcement, because the Spirit puts the law on the inside of us. Think of it as something like wet concrete. The law is the wooden form that holds the wet concrete in place.

Yet once the concrete "matures," once it firms up and holds its shape on its own, the wooden forms aren't needed anymore. As believers, we fulfill the law, but not because it constantly binds us like those wooden forms on wet concrete. Instead, we fulfill the law because we have absorbed the Spirit and the Word of God. It has become part of us, as though it is in our DNA, and so we seek to do the will of God because of the transformation that has happened to our hearts.

How I love these biblical truths. Yet as I write these words, I'm aware that what I am saying here might sound strange to many in our generation. I know this isn't what is commonly preached today. Yet I must say just as certainly that what I'm describing is the gospel as the Bible proclaims it. If it sounds odd to our ears, it is because we are used to a watered-down gospel and not the gospel of the Lord Jesus Christ. Let me explain.

I've been watching the church scene in the world for many years, particularly the church scene in the United States. We've undergone some pretty tremendous changes in recent decades, and much of it has been in the wrong direction. It all began, I suppose, when talk of being born again became popular back in the 1970s and 1980s. This was largely due to the influence of Jimmy Carter and Ronald Reagan. Both men spoke of being born again, and both were bold about the influence of Jesus Christ upon their lives. I was grateful that something I cared so much about was being openly discussed in our world. I was also grateful for the people I saw giving their lives to Jesus as a result.

Before long, though, our churches thought themselves too sophisticated, too mainstream to emphasize this business of being born again. We thought we were beyond all that conversion business. All of a sudden we had decisions instead of conversions. We had other things on our minds. For many Christians, the cross became not a death to this world and its ways, but rather an entitlement to all this world has to offer. There were also weird theological extremes. People began to say that since God was going to make them go to heaven whether they chose to or not, it didn't matter what they did in the flesh. They claimed that it had no bearing on their salvation.

All of this converged to make an entirely new kind of church experience. No longer were churches focused upon calling people to repentance. The very idea became an insult. Churches became about making better moral people. They also became about motivating people to happy living, about helping believers believe in themselves. I was stunned by how rapidly the change occurred. I remember visiting some of my friends' churches and seeing that there were no altars. I would ask them, "Where do you pray for people? Where do conversions happen?" The look on their faces told the story. It was as though they wanted to say, "What conversions? What repentance?"

Frankly, it was tragic, and it still is. Some wise scholars have said that we live in an era of "moralistic therapeutic deism."[11] They are right. People are intensely focused upon morality, though it often isn't the morality of God. They are interested in getting the help for their souls that they think they need, though this help is often emotional and not spiritual. It is certainly not a matter of help from the living God. And it is all awash with deism, which is the belief that God started the world and He'll come back to judge it one day, but that He really isn't very involved in the world in the meantime.

That pretty much captures where we are. I'm reminded of the way the eminent scholar H. Richard Niebuhr described theological liberalism in his epic book *The Kingdom of God in America*. He said liberalism taught that "a God without wrath brought men without sin into a kingdom without judgment through the ministrations of a Christ without a cross."[12] That certainly describes the church in America and much of the world today. We've forsaken the true gospel.

What we need is a return of the life-changing gospel of Jesus Christ. We need the kind of gospel Dwight Moody preached in the last century. He said he preached the three Rs: "ruin by sin, redemption by Christ, and regeneration by the Holy Spirit."[13]

We need the kind of gospel I grew up with. We were certain of what we believed. We knew we had been born into sin. We knew, and I know today, that Jesus Christ was sent by the Father in heaven. I knew that Jesus died on the cross to pay my penalty for sin. He redeemed me, gave me His Spirit, and now He calls me to come and learn His ways. It is a process. I'm not perfect, and I don't believe I will be in this life. But I will be His, and I am right now. I know whose I am and to whom I belong. It has made all the difference.

That is the gospel. Yet because we have turned to happy motivational talk and accommodation of the world in our churches, we are trying to make the gospel something different entirely. We are trying to change the gospel from the call to a transformed heart and a spirit of power that enables us to live up to God's standards, and make it into a self-help philosophy that allows us to live as we please and call it grace.

I scanned some Christian magazines and blogs recently to see what big ethical and moral dilemmas are being discussed. I wanted to know what Christians were regarding as challenges today.

I couldn't believe what I saw. In one youth-oriented magazine, there was a big discussion that essentially came down to whether it was OK for Christians to cuss. Another magazine article and related blogs debated whether Christians are allowed to smoke marijuana. Premarital sex came in for fairly soft treatment in a few publications, and everything I read indicated that the church of Jesus Christ has simply given up on opposing most behaviors that a generation ago were considered immoral. More tragic still, when I reviewed printed sermons and podcasts of sermons, I found almost none of these issues being confronted from pulpits that were aflame with righteousness. Preachers seem to have caved in. They seem more intent upon drawing large crowds with misty-eyed happy talk. It is a horrendous state of affairs. And it is no wonder that in this environment people are trying to stretch the grace of God into permission from God to do whatever they want.

My point is that much of the gospel can no longer be found in the church in our time. That is why when I say that being born again should mean a Spirit-empowered remaking of the human heart toward the goal of fulfilling the will of God, it sounds to some Christians as if I am from Mars. They simply haven't heard anything like it before.

Much of the law and grace debate in our time is simply a debate over what the gospel is. Do we believe "the faith which was once delivered to the saints,"[14] or do we embrace trendy, watered-down, motivational talk? Do we preach a costly gospel that calls for repentance and a life of surrender, or do we commit to the materialistic, self-centered pabulum of most churches today? Do we build upon the Bible, or do we build upon the shifting sands of modern culture?

I'm for the gospel of Jesus—the hard-core, unvarnished gospel of the risen Christ. And because I am for that gospel and no other, I do not believe it abolishes the moral law of God. I believe this glorious message proclaims a Jesus who fulfilled the law and who now empowers us to live for the glory of God. I believe in truths passed through the cross, tempered by grace, covered in mercy and still confronting the believer with works ordained by God. I do not believe in a salvation earned by works. I do believe in a salvation that calls for appropriate action as an offering to a loving God. When we return to that gospel, we will find the message of hyper-grace fleeing before a message of costly grace and a people holy, full of godly passion, and eager to please their Lord.

That's where you'll find me.

# CHAPTER 7

# Conduct That Pleases the Lord

*Being a Christian is more than just
an instantaneous conversion—it is
a daily process whereby you grow
to be more and more like Christ.*

—BILLY GRAHAM

W E HAVE LEARNED, then, that the law of God passes through the cross and gives us principles for living. We have also learned that the Holy Spirit works in us to fashion us into the image of Jesus, to empower and enable us to fulfill God's perfect will for our lives.

Now that we are sure of these truths, we need to examine the great New Testament principles that are meant to govern our conduct. We couldn't have done this until we confronted the issue of our hearts, because these glorious truths are all about our hearts. They are principles—we really should just call them laws—that a people of sanctified hearts are meant to live by. Even though I have held them in reserve until now, I believe these principles or laws give us final answers for most of the great questions about law and grace. Frankly, most Christians miss these laws when they read the Bible, but I'm hoping that once you see them, you'll agree that they are God's wisdom distilled for us so that we can live lives that are both pleasing to the Lord and fruitful in the world.

I love these truths because they move the whole debate about law and grace to a higher plane. Most of the big ethical issues that people argue about when it comes to law and grace have to do with low-level motives. Do I have the right to do a certain thing? Am I free to act in a certain way? Who has the authority to tell me I can't do what I want? Aren't I free in Christ to do whatever I please? And those on the more law-oriented side of the discussion also speak about fairly low-level matters. Is it allowed? Isn't a certain thing off-limits? Won't God be mad if I do that? These questions and their answers really don't point us to the higher concerns and motives that should guide our lives. In fact, most of these questions don't give us wisdom for living at all. With that said, let's consider the great transforming principles for our conduct that arise from the counsel of the New Testament. I trust you'll find that law and grace converge beautifully in these marvelous truths.

To understand the great principles of Christian conduct in the New Testament, we have to understand something of the crises that were confronting the first-century church. I've often heard Christians speak of the early church as though it were perfect. In fact, whole denominations have been created with the sole intent of returning to "first-century purity." I love the fledgling church we read about in the New Testament. I love it the way you love the beginning of anything you hold dear. But it wasn't perfect, and it wasn't pure.

I know this because the Bible tells me so. In fact, the early church had problems that would shock most

Christians today. It's right there on the pages of the Book of Acts and Paul's letters to the churches. What would you do if your church held a Communion service and people showed up drunk? How would you feel if recently converted women shouted questions out to their husbands in the middle of a worship service? How would it affect your relationship with your local assembly if a man had an affair with his father's wife, or groups of believers split over whether they should be Jewish or Gentile in their approach to Christianity? What about if two believers in your church sued each other, or a whole group of people who thought they were prophets all prophesied loudly at the same time during a Sunday morning service? All of these problems and more troubled the early church leaders.

We should be thankful that we have the chance to learn from these early leaders as they confronted these unusual problems with the wisdom of the Holy Spirit. God's wisdom is on display in the Bible! Paul had to provide guidance to the churches under his care, and we get a front-row seat to it all, allowing us to learn the magnificent principles of Christian conduct the Lord revealed to Paul in the midst of dealing with those problems.

Strangely, one of the issues that caused Paul the most trouble is something that many Christians today can scarcely fathom. It was the matter of meat sacrificed to idols. I certainly understand why Christians reading the Bible today would be tempted to pass this subject by entirely. It just doesn't seem relevant to us. After all, none of us go to the local grocery store and have to decide what to do when we walk up to the "meat sacrificed to idols" section. Yet this was a huge point of contention for Paul and the believers of his time. We see verse after verse devoted to this problem in the New Testament—in fact, nearly an entire chapter of both the Book of Romans and the Book of 1 Corinthians deals with it. As Paul deals with this crisis, he expounds on some wonderful principles that apply to our conduct as well.

It makes perfect sense that Paul had to deal with this troublesome problem of conscience in the church at Rome and the church at Corinth. Both of these cities were filled with pagan temples, priests, altars, and worship. This is what led to the crisis that Paul found himself addressing again and again. In the first-century world, animal sacrifices to many different gods were common. In many cases, once an animal had been sacrificed on a pagan altar, the meat of that animal could be sold in the marketplace, and thus served in private homes. Some Christians apparently bought this meat and served it to their families. Others found themselves as guests in pagan homes or at official banquets in which meat sacrificed to idols was served.

We can imagine how this might have become a problem in the churches. It probably happened just as it would today. After church one day one believer tells another of the banquet they attended the night before, and they mention that the meat served was from the sacrifices at the temple of Apollo. Or perhaps one housewife told another that the meat sacrificed to Aphrodite was a particularly good value in the market this week. The news would stun the other housewife, who would be scandalized by the thought of a Christian eating meat sacrificed to a demon. That's what the early Christians thought all the pagan gods were: demons. So you can see why this was such an outrage in the minds of some Christians.

Then as now, the Christians who couldn't agree about the matter would appeal to their pastors. These pastors, needing help in dealing with this question, would appeal to their apostolic leaders, and this is what caused Paul to address the problem repeatedly.

As Paul laid down guidelines about meat sacrificed to idols, he gave us wisdom that relates to everything from what movies we should see to the clothes we should wear, and from how we should speak to how we should vote.

There are seven principles Paul touches upon as he speaks to this matter. Let's make sure we pay close attention to each one of them.

### 1. The law of love

When we listen to Paul on the subject of meat sacrificed to idols, it becomes immediately clear that his greatest concern is love. In 1 Corinthians 8, one of the chapters of the New Testament devoted to this issue, Paul begins immediately by establishing that love, and not knowledge, should rule in our hearts, our speech, and our conduct. He writes, "Now as concerning food offered to idols: We know that 'we all have knowledge.' Knowledge produces arrogance, but love edifies."[1]

Paul establishes much the same emphasis in his other chapter on meat sacrificed to idols, Romans 14. There he writes, "If your brother is grieved because of your food, you are no longer walking in love. Do not destroy with your food one for whom Christ died."[2]

By emphasizing love as the basis for Christian conduct, Paul establishes a principle for us that applies to a thousand other matters: the law of love. He makes clear that he does not think that meat is unclean when it has been sacrificed to idols: "I know and am persuaded by the Lord Jesus that nothing is unclean in itself."[3] Yet he also recognizes that not everyone feels the same way: "but to him who considers anything to be unclean, to him it is unclean."[4] His conclusion is that each person should be guided by what is best for others. This is what love would do. This is how love conducts itself.

It is a powerful truth that we should hold deeply at heart. Much of the law and grace debate today is centered on what Christians have the "right" or the "freedom" to do. Paul isn't putting up with that. He specifically says that if love rules, rights have to be surrendered. Liberty has to bow to what is best for others. This is what love does. This is what Jesus would do.

Listen to how Paul unfolds this: "Therefore let us no longer pass judgment on one another, but rather determine not to put a stumbling block or an obstacle in a brother's way."[5] "For the kingdom of God does not mean eating and drinking, but righteousness and peace and joy in the Holy Spirit. For he who serves Christ in these things is acceptable to God and approved by men."[6] "Do not destroy the work of God for the sake of food. All things indeed are clean, but it is evil for the man who causes someone to fall by what he eats. It is good neither to eat meat nor drink wine, nor do anything whereby your brother stumbles or is offended or is made weak."[7]

It is an awe-inspiring thing to see how the law of love cuts so cleanly. While people in the first century and people today are preoccupied with their rights, the law of love turns the entire discussion around. The question ceases to be what I have the right to do in Christ, and it becomes a matter of what I should do for the good of others. This is the way of the Lord, and it applies to many other matters. Listen to the way Paul expressed this: "'All things are lawful for me,' but not all things are helpful. 'All things are lawful for me,' but not all things edify. Let no one seek his own, but each one the other's well-being."[8]

We can apply this law of love to a huge number of practical situations. Suppose I am going to a movie with friends. Let's say the movie is free of the bad language and sex that so many movies have today, but it also has a good deal of violence in it. Suppose one of my friends really struggles with this issue. Perhaps he comes from a violent background and has problems keeping bloody images from troubling his mind. Should we go to the movie, though it would pose no moral or spiritual problems for the rest of those going? The law of love answers that we should not go, because even though it may not bother most of us, not going is best for one of us. We don't want to destroy our friend's conscience. Two hours of entertainment is not worth the damage that would be done.

We should think about this law of love in all we do. It applies to the most practical decisions in our lives. Does Susie have the right to wear that fashionable new dress? Not if it is so revealing that it causes her Christian brothers to stumble. Does Bill have the right to talk tough to his athlete friend? It may not cause a problem for him or his friend, but it may mean that an admiring younger man sees his example and thinks it is all right to engage in swearing and coarse talk. The question always seems to be, "Am I allowed to do that?" The question we should be asking is, "Why would I want to do that when others' lives and consciences are going to be negatively affected?"

At the heart of our conduct should not be the ever-pressing demand for our rights. It should be the ever-pressing demands of love for others. In one short principle Paul—and more importantly, the Holy Spirit—turns the entire debate about Christian rights on its head. And He makes us more like Jesus in the process.

## 2. The law of faith

In Paul's writing about this matter of meat sacrificed to idols, he continually mentions the core matter of faith. He makes it very clear that just as our approach to this subject must be one of love, it must also be grounded in faith. In fact, Paul goes so far as to say that what we don't do in faith is actually sin. Consider these various statements about faith and conduct that we find in Romans 14.

> Welcome him who is weak in faith, but not for the purpose of arguing over opinions. For one has faith to eat all things, but he who is weak eats only vegetables.[9]

> But he who doubts is condemned if he eats, because it is not from faith, for whatever is not from faith is sin.[10]

Paul establishes another important principle here. It is the law of faith. What he means is that our conduct should proceed from our faith—from what we believe as Christians—but also from our certainties about God and His will. If we are not confident that our conduct proceeds from our faith, and if we have doubts as we involve ourselves in disputable matters, then Paul says we are engaging in sin.

This means that if we cannot watch a movie in faith, then we shouldn't watch it, no matter its rating or its topic. It means that if we repeat a joke we have heard, and we are uncertain and doubting the rightness of it as we do, then we shouldn't repeat it. Paul says that what does not come from faith in these matters is sin. The same is true of the books we read, the kinds of places we frequent, the way we talk, the way we dress, and innumerable other categories of behavior. If we can't do it with assurance that it meets with God's approval, it is not being done in faith and is not pleasing to God. In other words, we have our answer about what is right or wrong regardless of what others do. If it isn't faith for us, it isn't right for us.

Let me give you a brief and unusual example of how this can work. I have a friend who is a historian. He is a solid, happy Christian who lives life to the full. He isn't the retreating, fearful type who runs from every shadow in the world. He's bold and passionate and serious about the things of God.

He surprised me one day when he told me that he has never gone to the circus. I couldn't believe it. Given his personality, I thought a circus would be just the kind of thing this friend would enjoy with friends and family. The reason he has never gone to circuses is that he can't do it in faith. His historian gifts make him so aware of the Christians killed in Roman circuses that, for him, it is as though it happened yesterday. My friend just can't go with confidence that it is the right thing for him to do.

It is important for you to understand that my friend doesn't think it is wrong for Christians to go to the circus. Not at all. He's glad for others to enjoy that form of entertainment all they want. They can do it in faith. He can't. So without being legalistic or judgmental about it, he won't go to a circus. He just can't do it in faith and so, for him, it would be sin.

That's how it works, and how it should work for all of us. The law of faith, like the law of love, is a measuring rod for our conduct. It helps us align our lives with the will of God and the counsel of the Holy Spirit within us.

### 3. The law of liberty

It is fascinating that in Paul's writings about a contentious issue within the early church, he doesn't just crack down on the saints in legalism, but he establishes a principle that we desperately need in our day. He defines for us the law of Christian liberty.

It might easily have gone the other way. How much easier it would have been for Paul to simply say, "Listen, no meat sacrificed to idols. Not ever. This is the rule for all our churches, and I don't want to hear any more about it."

But that's not what Paul does. Instead, he goes to great pains to establish that people are free to believe differently about things, and he even makes it clear that people are free to disagree with him and not be wrong to do so. Read carefully how he lays this foundation of liberty.

> Do not let him who eats despise him who does not eat, and do not let him who does not eat judge him who eats, for God has welcomed him. Who are you to judge another man's servant? To his own master he stands or falls. And he will stand, for God is able to make him stand. One man judges one day above another; another judges every day alike. Let each one be fully persuaded in his own mind. He who observes the day observes it for the Lord, and he who does not observe the day, to the Lord he does not observe it. He who eats, eats in honor of the Lord, for he gives thanks to God; and the one who does not eat, in honor of the Lord he does not eat, and gives thanks to God.[11]

> So why do you judge your brother? Or why do you despise your brother?[12]

> Therefore let us no longer pass judgment on one another, but rather determine not to put a

stumbling block or an obstacle in a brother's way. I know and am persuaded by the Lord Jesus that nothing is unclean in itself, but to him who considers anything to be unclean, to him it is unclean.[13]

When I read these words, I often think of the modern critics who accuse Paul of being a moral dictator. They charge that Paul hated women and was anti-marriage and that he went far beyond anything Jesus intended when it comes to personal freedom.

These liberal critics just haven't read the Bible! In the words above, we see that Paul is allowing a vast amount of individual freedom of belief. On an entire array of matters Paul establishes that each man must decide for himself and before the Lord.

Thank God for this law of liberty. Without it, we would have to excommunicate every Christian who doesn't believe as we do. We would live in fear of disagreements with our Christian friends because it would always mean contention and separation. Instead, we can disagree even within the same church, even within the same family or band of friends, and still serve the Lord in love and unity.

Some matters are firmly established by Scripture. Those that aren't, those issues that Paul calls "disputable" or "uncertain," are left to believers to decide for themselves as they have been given the light of revelation to decide before the Lord. This is one of the great truths of the Christian faith, and I think we should all thank God for it.

### 4. The law of conscience

Paul often mentions conscience in his writing. In fact, it is a topic he applies to a wide variety of issues. His main objective in all this is what is described in 1 Peter 3:21 as "a clear conscience toward God" (NIV).

The word *conscience* refers to an inner knowing of what is right. The word in the original language literally means co-knowledge. It is the part of our hearts or our inner man that confirms the will of God, that bears witness to or affirms agreement with what is right.

We can see why Paul places such emphasis on this matter of conscience. He teaches in his writings that our conscience can be corrupted. He urges us to have a "good conscience,"[14] that comes from "having our hearts sprinkled to cleanse us from a guilty conscience."[15] He stands against false teachers who have "seared" consciences,[16] but he constantly reassures his readers by saying that his "conscience confirms" that he has conducted himself properly.[17]

So Paul understands the power of a good conscience, and he tells us that our conscience should determine our conduct. I call this the law of conscience. We should act in agreement with our conscience in all we do. Our conscience should not condemn us and should not convict us or make us uneasy about our actions.

What I'm describing here is more than a feeling or a hunch. It involves making choices according to the sense on the inside that we are doing what is right according to God's standards and character. Your conscience is like a moral GPS. You want to pay attention to it so you take the right path in life.

This matter of conscience is so important that Paul even says that when people of weak conscience won't eat certain foods, when we are with them we shouldn't eat those foods either, because we don't want to violate their conscience. Here we see the law of love and the law of conscience working together.

> But take heed, lest by any means this liberty of yours becomes a stumbling block to those who are weak. For if anyone sees you, who have knowledge, eating in the idol's temple, shall the conscience of him who is weak not be emboldened to eat those things which are offered to idols, and by your knowledge shall the weak brother perish, for whom Christ died? When you thus sin against the brothers, wounding their weak conscience, you sin against Christ.[18]

Clearly this law of conscience is nothing to trifle with. We must consult our own conscience in deciding about our actions, and we must not trample the conscience of others. Paul could not issue a stronger warning about this. He says that to do so is to "sin against Christ."

## 5. The law of offering

Another emphasis that Paul establishes in his writings about meat sacrificed to idols has to do with how we conduct ourselves "as to the Lord." Paul presents this attitude, or this orientation, as a guide to how we should live.

Listen to what he tells us in Romans 14:6–8.

> He who observes the day observes it for the Lord, and he who does not observe the day, to the Lord he does not observe it. He who eats, eats in honor of the Lord, for he gives thanks to God; and the one who does not eat, in honor of the Lord he does not eat, and gives thanks to God. For none of us lives for himself, and no one dies for himself. For if we live, we live for the Lord. And if we die, we die for the Lord. So, whether we live or die, we are the Lord's.

Here we have another guiding principle that I call the law of offering. The Bible tells us that we are to offer our lives as an offering to God. As Paul wrote in Romans 12:1, we are to surrender ourselves "as a living sacrifice, holy, and acceptable to God, which is your reasonable service of worship." This, of course, is the call of every Christian—the definition of the normal Christian life.

Yet in Paul's writings about food sacrificed to idols, he uses the fact that our lives are to be lived "unto the Lord" as a kind of gyroscope to help us make decisions about our conduct. Repeatedly the measure of a man's actions is whether he can do what he plans to do "unto the Lord." In other words, can he offer what he is doing as an offering to the Lord? Are his actions a holy sacrifice to God?

This law of offering is a powerful guide to our behavior. I mentioned earlier that I read an article debating whether Christians can smoke marijuana. The whole argument was centered on whether Christians have the liberty to smoke pot. Let me join Paul in realigning the debate. Let me ask if any Christian anywhere can claim that they can smoke marijuana, other than possibly for a medical purpose, as an offering to God or, in Paul's words, "as unto the Lord." I doubt it. And that article I read about what cuss words are allowed for Christians? Try using that foul language "as unto the Lord," or as an offering to God. The whole case for cursing falls away. No one who worships Jesus as Lord would ever curse in His face. It just wouldn't happen, and we all know it. This is the clarity that the law of offering brings to us.

This is a principle that we should pull to the center of our lives. If there is anything we are doing that we would never do "as unto the Lord," then we should not do it. This truth cuts finely. I have a friend who loves football. He can easily watch the Super Bowl with his family and do so as unto the Lord without a problem. Yet every year, when the halftime show begins, he and his family turn off the television. They can't watch all the lustful images to the glory of God. But when the halftime show is over and the second half begins, they turn the television on again.

Are these friends of mine weird? No, they are just believers in Jesus who want to live their lives as offerings to the Lord. I admire them. In fact, I fully intend to be just like them. We should all desire to live according to Paul's law of offering.

## 6. The law of peace

This next law does not arise from the specific language Paul uses in discussing disputes about food and holy days, but it does seem to be part of his broad conclusion. I call it the law of peace. It is probably best summarized in Philippians 4:7: "And the peace of God, which surpasses all understanding, will protect your hearts and minds through Christ Jesus." That word *protect* is probably better translated "govern" or even "referee." In other words, the peace of God should be a deciding force in your heart and mind as you live before God.

In all the places in the New Testament where Paul talks about this controversy—Romans 14, 1 Corinthians 8, and 1 Corinthians 10 among them—he seems to establish a guiding principle of peace. *If you are at peace with your decision, if you are preserving peace with your brother or sister, and if you are at peace with God, then you are free to act.*

The point is that peace is a guide to us. It referees over our decisions. It leads us. It helps us govern our passions and determine the right course. Perhaps you've heard Christians say to each other, "Do you have peace about your decision?" or "What does your peace tell you?" This is exactly in line with Paul's approach to both individual decisions and to controversial issues in the church. What does peace dictate? This is not cowardice of the kind that seeks peace in all situations only because it fears and avoids conflict. That isn't godly. We should always be ready to risk conflict when we follow Jesus. Rather, I'm talking about peace from God that rules and controls your heart when you are certain you are taking a correct course of action. I'm talking about a force of peace and certainty that comes from God when we live righteously before Him.

Let us keep this law close to our hearts as well. There is a law of peace that we should consult in all our ways. If we feel no peace when we act, we should stop and reconsider. The peace of God will settle on us when we act in holiness and walk the path God has ordained. I consider this truth one of the great principles of the Christian life, and it has helped me since my youth. Thank God for His peace.

### 7. The law of certainty

Finally, there is a truth that Paul emphasizes in the midst of crisis that will probably surprise more than a few believers. I call it the law of certainty, and I can tell you that it is nearly the opposite of what is considered acceptable today.

Have you noticed that being indecisive, uncertain, and nervous has almost become a style these days? It is as though we are all supposed to be neurotic—always talking fast, always confused, ever uncertain, and constantly nervous as a result. This new trend may be a preferred behavior among young folks, but it isn't what springs naturally from a Christian life lived in the Holy Spirit.

We all experience periods of uncertainty, and there is no sin in that. However, when we are pondering the path our lives should take or the manner in which we should conduct ourselves, Paul says that a certainty of heart is part of the confirmation that we are on the right road.

In Romans, Paul insists that no matter what a person considers to be true about food or sacred days, each one should be "fully persuaded in his own mind."[19] Similarly, he says that in the matter of food sacrificed to idols, "he who doubts is condemned if he eats, because it is not from faith."[20] All of this sounds very much like the words the Holy Spirit gave to the apostle James: "But when you ask, you must believe and not doubt, because the one who doubts is like a wave of the sea, blown and tossed by the wind. That person should not expect to receive anything from the Lord. Such a person is double-minded and unstable in all they do."[21]

Obviously, when we are on the right path—when we are walking in love, our conscience approves our steps, and we have peace that we are doing the right thing—we should have the confirmation of certainty. By this I don't mean arrogance or stubbornness. We've had enough of that kind of counterproductive posturing in the Christian world. I'm talking about the calm, solid certainty that comes from knowing you are doing the right thing. In the same way that peace should *lead* us to right decisions, certainty should *result* from our right decisions.

And let me tell you that I don't care how stylish it may seem to be nervous and uncertain in our generation, there is nothing as attractive as a man or a woman walking in humble righteous certainty.

So these then are the great principles of Christian conduct that arise from that tumultuous period in the early church. I'm grateful for each one of these laws. They have seen me in good stead throughout my life, and they still guide me today.

What I want you to take with you from this list is that many of the issues that get bound up in the law and grace debate would never arise among a people observing the principles I've described here. Most of the debate would just melt away because the matter of love or peace or offering our lives to the Lord or conscience or faith would cut the issue down like a terrible swift sword.

Trust me in this. We are having debates about our rights and privileges because we have not embraced the cross, we have not read our Bibles, and we have not let the principles of God temper our desires. When we do, we will live in both peace and prosperity and we will, finally, become a people of both law and grace who will attract the attention of those who are confused, broken, and overlooked in this fallen world.

# CHAPTER 8

# Government and Glory

*Grace means undeserved kindness. It is the gift of God to man the moment he sees he is unworthy of God's favor.*

—Dwight L. Moody

W E LIVE IN a world of extremes. Today it is common for two things that should be in harmonious synchronization with one another to be presented as constantly at odds. This tension is all around us. We view the artist and the accountant as though they are opposites, when in fact they need each other. We speak of the thoughtful person and the emotional person as though they are always at war. In the same way, the extrovert and the introvert have recently been highlighted in popular literature, but always as though they must be in dire conflict. It just isn't true. Our lives would be diminished without the differences and even the opposites that we encounter in one another. What we need is for those who find themselves at opposing ends of an issue to learn to blend together.

The same is true of structure and spirit, or as I like to say it, government and glory, in the modern church. Both are of equal necessity, just as we need the benefits of both law and grace. If the adversary of our souls can be successful in keeping us divided into opposing camps, our efforts to accomplish God's will and purpose in the earth will be frustrated. I believe—in fact,

I know—that there is an answer. But first let's analyze and illustrate the problem from another perspective.

Some issues are too large to be ignored, but they lie under the surface, and it can be tempting to believe they don't exist. The San Andreas Fault runs beneath some of the largest metropolitan areas in the state of California, yet millions of its citizens live there every day without giving a thought about the disastrous effects of the next big shock. But let an earthquake or a tremor occur, and multiplied thousands will become aware of the ominous possibility of their homes or even their entire communities being torn asunder. In much the same way, there is a divide in the church that, left unchecked, threatens our souls and our mission in the world of men. There is a deep and widening division in the body of Christ that has taken place between those who emphasize the Word of God as opposed to those who desire nothing but the Spirit of God. (And of course, I am mindful that there are many who attend church who want neither!)

I contend that the church can only be an effective agent of redemptive change in our families and neighborhoods, our communities and the broader culture at large, if and when we are both grounded in God's Word and saturated with and moving in the Holy Spirit. Both of these are absolutely essential for a revival to take place in our hearts and the world that will be undeniable, uncontrollable, and unstoppable.

One can easily discern this division among the people of God by simple observation of their conversations. On the Word side, the rhetoric might be, "We need more Bible teaching on fundamentals of the faith such as the substitutionary sacrifice of Jesus Christ, His resurrection, the second coming, divine healing, God's sovereignty, the authority of the believer, and many other foundational truths."

On the Spirit side, the conversation would lean toward statements such as, "We need more jubilant praise and deep worship, more emotional expression and energy, more signs, wonders, and gifts of the Holy Ghost and demonstrations of the power of God in operation. These were hallmarks of the church in the Book of Acts, and they should be in evidence now."

The question is, Which of these is correct, or of greater importance? It's my conviction that this distinction of emphasis may not be overt at all. Often Satan's greatest victories are accomplished with the slightest diversions accumulating over time. I don't believe it is proper to ask any believer to actually choose between the Word and Spirit, or government and glory. Most Christians would assuredly agree that both are necessary to properly represent our great God to a world in need. However, I also believe the Bible gives us very clear guidance in regard to which of these concepts needs to be given first priority.

Here is a clue about which of these is of foremost

significance, from John 1:1: "In the beginning was the Word, and the Word was with God, and the Word was God." Here is another, from Psalm 138:2: "You have exalted Your word above all Your name."

We tend to think of words mainly as expressions of ideas. But when God has an idea, He is not limited to giving expression to it only in the form of words. God actually creates things as a result of His words. We see this throughout the creation narrative in Genesis. God had a thought, or a concept, and made it a manifest reality by merely speaking it into existence. It was not; but then God said it, and it came into being so that it could be observed in the natural realm.

Beyond this, Hebrews 1:3 shouts that God, through Jesus Christ, the living Word, "upholds all things by the word of His power." He not only created the universe and everything in it by His word, He also maintains all things by His word.

None of this is meant to diminish the importance of God's name. God first revealed His name to Moses, in Exodus 6:3: "I appeared to Abraham, to Isaac, and to Jacob as God Almighty [El-Shaddai], but by My name the Lord [Yahweh—the redemptive name of God] I did not make Myself known to them" (AMPC). God's name represents His authority, which gives rise to great spiritual manifestations and demonstrations of His glory. Jesus authorized us to use His name to accomplish His will. This is made evident in the Great Commission:

He said to them, "Go into all the world, and preach the gospel to every creature. He who believes and is baptized will be saved. But he who does not believe will be condemned. These signs will accompany those who believe: In My name they will cast out demons; they will speak with new tongues; they will take up serpents; if they drink any deadly thing, it will not hurt them; they will lay hands on the sick, and they will recover."[1]

It is of value to note that when the almighty God did choose to reveal His name to Moses, an outpouring of signs, wonders, miracles, and glorious manifestations and demonstrations followed. In fact, Moses was overwhelmed by the wonders God performed in his sight to convince him that he was truly chosen to go to Egypt and speak to Pharaoh. Abraham, Isaac, and Jacob saw supernatural things, but not to the same degree or in the same volume that accompanied the revelation of God's name to Moses and the children of Israel.

But we are not saved because we have seen signs, wonders, and miracles. Vast multitudes have seen all of those things and still have not believed God for their salvation. We are saved by hearing and believing the Word of God. That is the gospel. Signs and wonders may attract attention, but it is only through the proclamation of God's Word that people can be saved. Abraham is an outstanding example of faith in the Old

Testament, but even Abraham did not see the miracle of Isaac until after he put his trust and confidence in God's infallible Word.

God desires a relationship with us. He already knows us inside and out, but His will is for us to know Him. Any relationship, whether with God or with another person, takes time to develop. And one of the best ways to get to know someone, and whether or not we can trust them, is to find out what they have said. This takes time and diligent effort, which is one of the reasons relatively few people get to really know God. Regardless of how long you have been a Christian or what experiences you have had in the kingdom of God, there is no substitute for reading, studying, and applying God's Word, and spending time with Him in worship and prayer. This is fundamental and foundational to our growth and development as believers, and yet it is overlooked or ignored by many Christians.

A recent poll of pastors and church leaders revealed that on average they spend only a few minutes a day in personal worship and devotion in the presence of God. If that is the testimony of our leaders, how much time does an average believer spend with God each day? The reason we don't see the results Jesus did is because we don't do the things Jesus did. He spent time with His Father and received supernatural strength and divine direction because of it. How much of the modern church's weakness and confusion is because they are only experientially motivated and see no necessity of "studying to show themselves approved unto God"?[2]

Of course the resounding reply is, "But we're so very, very busy." We say we honor those we regard as giants of faith, but we refuse to emulate them. We allow other activities to replace deep devotional time in pursuit of the precepts and concepts of victorious lives found only like pearls in deep dives into God's infallible Word. Sometimes it is necessary to push your plate back or put down your cell phone and pick up a Bible.

Many church attenders crave only an experience that appeals to their emotions and makes them feel good, or a prophetic pronouncement of God's favor and blessing, or an extended passionate praise and worship service, but never seem to have the time, energy, or desire for personal pursuit of the revelation of God's Word for themselves.

Let me share with you some profound words from my wonderful wife, Joni. She has a tremendous way of expressing God's truths in simplistic terms:

> Do we seek relationship or experience? Relationship takes discipline marked by maturity, whereas experience is a one-night stand—all emotion and no investment. Where God is concerned, are we looking for goose bumps or a wedding band? One is based on feelings, and the other is based on faith. One is based on instant

gratification, and the other is based on a long-term commitment.

—FROM JONI'S JOURNAL, WEDNESDAY,
SEPTEMBER 7, 2011

God is not interested in being involved in our lives for just one night, or until a crisis has passed, or for a brief season. He is interested in a long-term relationship—one that lasts forever. Listen to how the prophet Isaiah tells it:

> For unto us a child is born, unto us a son is given, and the government shall be upon his shoulder. And his name shall be called Wonderful Counselor, Mighty God, Eternal Father, Prince of Peace. Of the increase of his government and peace there shall be no end, upon the throne of David and over his kingdom, to order it and to establish it with justice and with righteousness, from now until forever. The zeal of the LORD of Hosts will perform this.[3]

Concerning the coming Messiah, Isaiah said, "and the government shall be upon His shoulder." God plans to rule and reign eternally through the agency of His Son, Jesus Christ—not for a term or two, or for a decade, but forever. And we will have the incredible privilege of ruling and reigning with Him. But in order to rule, we must learn the principles of God's kingdom.

And one of the first rules is this, found in Psalm 103:19: "The LORD has established His throne in the heavens, and His kingdom rules over all."

God's providence is universal. There is nothing outside the scope of His authority. He created all, and therefore rules over all. While it is true that there are some who demonstrate rebellion now, eventually even the rebels will be required to acknowledge that there is One who rules and reigns over everything.

God has prepared His throne—it is fixed, it is established, it cannot be shaken. His government is foreordained and is forever. It is accomplished according to the counsel of His own will. There is no exempt jurisdiction from the government of God. He rules and reigns as sovereign and supreme over all.

Let me explain why this deserves such emphasis by quoting another prophet who was well acquainted with people who refused to recognize God's government, as evidenced by their rebellion and refusal to hear His words.

> Afterward he brought me to the gate, the gate facing east. And the glory of the God of Israel came from the way of the east. And His voice was like a noise of many waters. And the earth shone with His glory. It was according to the appearance of the vision which I saw, even according to the vision that I saw, when He came to destroy the city. And the visions were like the vision that

I saw by the River Kebar. And I fell upon my face. The glory of the LORD came into the temple by the way of the gate facing east. So the Spirit took me up and brought me into the inner court. And the glory of the LORD filled the temple.

Then I heard one speaking to me out of the temple. And a man stood by me. He said to me: Son of man, this is the place of My throne and the place of the soles of My feet, where I will dwell in the midst of the sons of Israel forever. And My holy name shall the house of Israel defile no more, nor they nor their kings by their harlotry, nor by the corpses of their kings when they die. By setting their threshold by My threshold and their post by My posts and the wall between Me and them, they have even defiled My holy name by their abominations that they have committed. Therefore I have consumed them in My anger. Now let them put away their harlotry and the corpses of their kings far from Me, and I will dwell in their midst forever.

As for you, son of man, describe the temple to the house of Israel, that they may be ashamed of their iniquities. And let them measure the pattern. If they are ashamed of all that they have done, show them the design of the temple and its fashion and exits and its entrances and all its forms and all its ordinances and all its laws. And write it in their sight so that they may keep its whole form and all its ordinances and do them.

> This is the law of the temple: The whole terri-
> tory on the top of the mountain all around shall
> be most holy. This is the law of the temple.[4]

Ezekiel saw this vision of the millennial temple, and later saw it measured in detail, so that he could describe it to the remnant of the captives of Israel. When the vision began, the house, or temple, was already standing in its place. Then the prophet saw the glory of God enter the temple from the east. Keep the order of events in mind here. The temple was firmly established, built upon its proper foundation. After this, God's presence, or glory, entered the temple. First came the house, or the government, and then came the Spirit, or glory, into the house.

This reminds me of another vision that Ezekiel had, recorded in Ezekiel 37. In this vision the prophet saw a valley of dry bones. Due to God's miraculous intervention and the prophet's obedience, the bones came together into a vast army. However, only after this army of bones wrapped in flesh had come together from their separate parts did the wind of God fill them with life. God's Spirit could not fill something that had not been prepared to receive an infilling of His power by coming into order, or government.

So it is with us, His people. Only after we have been obedient to His Word and complied with His commands can we be a body ready to receive His Spirit. Government comes first, then glory. God's Spirit will not descend in satisfying fullness until we have become a people who are prepared to receive Him. In Ezekiel 43:4–5, the glory of God returned to the temple that He had forsaken because of Israel's idolatry. But in verse 6, Ezekiel heard God speak to him out of the same temple that was now restored. This divine indwelling could only occur after the house had been put in order and purified by obedience to God's orders—His Word, His government. Ezekiel 43:12 says it twice: "This is the law of the temple."

The law builds the house, but grace fills the house. Once the temple is constructed, it is nothing but an empty building unless God comes and fills it. This reveals why we need both the law of God and the grace of God—grace that is uncovered, unfiltered, undeserved. We need both structure and Spirit to fulfill our purpose in showing forth the character and works of God to a desperate world. When these two principles come together in the church, we will see an explosion of demonstration such as has never before been witnessed. The world will not be able to avoid noticing—and being attracted to—what God is manifesting in our midst.

Here is one more illustration of this concept. If you scan through the Book of Exodus and also through the Book of Hebrews, you'll find that the tabernacle in the wilderness was based on the heavenly tabernacle that houses the throne room of God. This is why God told Moses to build the earthly tabernacle according to the pattern revealed to him about the heavenly one. It is also why Moses was commanded to be so painstakingly precise. You have, no doubt, felt like I have when reading page after page in Exodus about the tabernacle. Whole chapters are devoted to a single piece of furniture. Sometimes the text reads like an engineer's report, with poles of an exact length, cloth of exact color, and fasteners of exact design. It seems to go on forever. We have to remind ourselves that what we are reading is the Word of God. We also have to remember what God instructed His servant, Moses: "According to all that I show you—the pattern of the tabernacle and the pattern of all its furniture—you shall make it just so."[5]

God is giving Moses a heavenly download. He's revealing a detailed plan for a smaller, earthly version of His heavenly tabernacle.

It must be precise.

In fact, it isn't just the tabernacle and its furnishings that have to be precise. God also gives exacting instruction regarding such things as how to make anointing oil, how to build the camp, how to station the tribes, and a hundred other matters. All must be crafted, positioned, and engineered just so. God is an exacting God, and He wanted an exact tabernacle for His purpose.

Sometimes this takes on a rather humorous cast. In

Deuteronomy 23:12–14, God tells the Israelites how they should conduct themselves regarding latrines. He's very specific. And then He concludes, "For the LORD your God walks in the midst of your camp, to deliver you, and to defeat your enemies before you. Therefore, your camp must be holy, so that He does not see any indecent thing among you, and turn away from you." Don't ever doubt that God is a God of precision and structure. He gives His people instruction about the most detailed and intimate of matters.

The point is that we see page after page of Scripture completely devoted to the will of God for the tabernacle and for the life of Israel centered upon it.

Why such attention to detail? Why such precise structure? Why such specific government of Israel's life before God?

The reason is a profound one—so that God might display His glory. We gain more than a hint of this in those few words that I quoted about the latrines. God says make your latrines right. Why is it so important? God gave them the answer: "Because I move among you. Because I dwell in the camp of Israel. Because I am present. Because My glory must dwell upon you."[6] You see, God's government is the landing pad for His glory to be manifested. The government is required for the glory to reside.

And so it is in our personal lives as well. All the boundaries and absolutes and grace-tempered laws that we are to observe in order to be God's people are necessary because our lives must be aligned with His will. Adherence to His will is the price of His glory. If there is no obedience, no surrender, no observance of His commands, then there will be no glory. This is what we learn from the history of Israel. When the Israelites broke God's commands, the glory of God departed. The word they used was Ichabod. It was a term of grief. It meant the glory has departed. There were no sadder words in Israel's history.

This is an overlooked key to why we don't see the same works manifested among us that have been witnessed in the past. The modern church has insisted upon its rights and forsaken its responsibilities. Some have demanded their liberty but have forfeited God's presence in the process of obtaining it. On the other hand, others have demanded obedience to a system of works and laws that goes far beyond anything that our Father expects and then wondered why He would not bless their efforts with His presence and His power.

God forbid that "Ichabod" becomes the banner over the church in our generation. God forbid that word be placed over our lives either. We cry out for His glory. We can't live without His presence. We reach with our faith for our Father to dwell among us. We don't earn this by striving to accomplish works to conform to the law, but we do honor and invite God's presence with our offerings of obedience and holiness.

This is why the truth regarding the absolute cohesiveness between law and grace is indispensable. We must no longer be interested in winning a debate. We are not simply dealing with whether or not we have rights in Christ. Our search is much deeper than a selfish attempt to discover what we are free to do. We are dealing in the valuable merchandise of preparing the people of God for His mighty and glorious presence. May each of us that bear His name govern our ways so that His manifested glory may reside upon us, within us, and around us.

Let us be a people who fulfill His structure and are filled with His Holy Spirit—who represent His government and reflect His glory, who walk according to His law and accept His grace—so that the God of grace—uncovered, unfiltered, undeserved—may be exalted in all the earth.

# Quotes About Law and Grace

## From Rod Parsley

I HOPE I HAVE shown you in these pages that I take the matter of law and grace very seriously. I understand the damage that extremes are doing in our day, and I'm eager to help us all find biblical balance. I want to include some of the things I've said to my own congregation about this topic. In a sense, I want to take you into our services—and in some cases, into the great meetings I conduct—and let you "hear" the words as I've said them in the moment. I trust that what I've said will inspire and instruct you, and I hope you'll get some feel for how I take on this cutting-edge subject out there along the battle lines of faith.

> There was a time when fear of judgment made us work and work and work until we could work no more. But try as we may, work as we might, we still could never earn His acceptance! But now, by faith, through grace, we can put away the leg braces of the law and stand uprightly in His presence, crying, Abba!
> —RAISE THE STANDARD PASTORS' CONFERENCE

> Let's hang up a new sign. Let's raise a new standard for a new generation. That banner says, "Send me your broken! Send me your huddled masses! Send me those yearning to breathe free!" That banner says, "Come, all that will

come, and drink of the river of the water of life freely!" This banner says, "Come unto me if you cut your body! Come unto me if you've had too much to drink! Send the homosexuals! Send the lesbians! Send those that are cursed! Send the drunkards! Send the pornographers! Send the prostitutes!" God is not mad at you. He never has been, and you don't have to do anything to try to make Him "unmad," because at this very moment, He's pursuing you with a fervent desire fueled by a Father's furious love to receive you— no longer as a servant, working for wages, but as His own child. Join me in Martin Luther's cry that sparked the greatest Reformation the world has ever known, "The just shall live by faith."

—Raise the Standard Pastors' Conference


We don't understand grace. We change the words of great theological hymns like "Amazing grace, how sweet the sound." We sing, "That saved a wretch like me." But we've got prominent preachers on television changing the words of historically correct and theologically correct hymns and teaching congregations to sing, "Amazing grace, how sweet the sound that saved someone like me." You see how the deterioration of true Bible doctrine leaves us weak and impotent? I'm not someone. I'm a sinner. Saved by grace, yes, but let's please understand what that means.

—Sermon, "What Grace Can and Cannot Do"

The law is unalterable. You cannot change the law. The only thing you can do with the law is answer it with a higher law. There was a law called sin and death. It was coursing through my veins. I wanted to do good and I couldn't. I wanted to do right and I couldn't. Then came a higher law. It was the law of grace and mercy in Christ Jesus.

—Sermon, "Grace"

Secular humanism has so permeated the preaching of modern pulpits that we can no longer recognize them from a psychology class at the local community college. The Bible shouts, "If in this life only we have peace with God, we are of all men most miserable." Yet we think we are entitled. We think we have a right to something for nothing! May I share with you that the Bible said the gift of God is eternal life? We have misunderstood the gifts of God for the debts of God. God owes us nothing! Our righteousness is as filthy rags. Our good works are but filthy rags. Our good attempts, our faithful attitudes, our attempts at religiosity, our marching to the cadence and creeds of creation are nothing but vain attempts to tell God we believe we're entitled. God said, "You want to live? Die. You want to receive? Give." Everything in His kingdom is mutually exclusive and diametrically opposed to everything in the kingdom you came out of.

And what we try to do is we try to drag that secular humanistic new age crystal-licking philosophy, and put it in the pulpit, and perpetrate it upon the pew! But it's not the gospel of Jesus Christ!

—SERMON, "PRODIGAL, BEFORE YOU LEAVE HOME"

The only sin God cannot forgive is unrepented sin. I don't believe that grace is going to cover my unrepented sin any more than I believe I could have been born again without repentance. The cross restored my ability to choose, and so I choose to repent, I choose to resist sin, I choose to declare war on my lusts. This is what it means to walk in the grace of Jesus. He offers us the power to take a stand for righteousness for ourselves.

—INTERVIEW

Martin Luther said, "We must know it is one thing to handle the subject of good works, and it is another thing entirely that of justification by faith, just as the nature of an individual is one thing, and his works are another." Your nature is one thing; your works are another. Justification has reference to the person and not to the works, which is contrary to everything most people hear every Sunday morning of the world, a focus on the works and not the person. It is the person,

said Luther, it is the person and not the works
which is justified and saved.

—Sermon, "A People of Law and Grace"

Relying solely on the straw armor of natural
light and the ability to reason, and human inge-
nuity, and human power, and human prowess,
the voices of our generation introduced their
heathen books and the doctrines of men, saying
that good works precede justification. In fact,
they said, men are made by the good works they
perform. They even quoted Aristotle, who said,
"He who does much good will thereby become
good." But this very doctrine that the anti-God,
anti-Christ, anti-church secular humanists
pervert has become the truth of God in many
churches today. They teach that God must first
respect the works and then the doer. This satanic
lie, this deceptive intellectual spirit rules and
reigns universally at this very moment in the
hallowed halls of higher education and the local
public school, and it also is paramount in the
pulpits of America, as preachers have become
nothing more than Dr. Phil wannabes dribbling
out dime store pop psychology as though it was
Holy Ghost–inspired Bible truth!

They commit spiritual adultery and scriptural
rape by telling the undiscerning masses that if
we just feel good about ourselves and do good
works, we're going to make it to heaven.

The advocates of such diabolical deception are but Cain-like imitators of true saints, and they are disregarded of God Himself! You might ask Luther how you can secure that kind of justification. The Bible replies to you, "Hear Christ, believe Him utterly, despairing of yourself, and your self-righteousness, and your self-worth and resting completely, assured in Christ alone. You will be changed! You can be transformed from a Cain to an Abel. Faith is justification!"

—Sermon, "A People of Law and Grace"

There is a distinction to be drawn between saving and keeping (living) grace. Again, grace is not the absence of law any more than peace is the absence of war. The curse of the law is not that the law is cursed but in our previous inability to keep it.

—Sermon, "Kingdom > Culture"

# FAMOUS QUOTES

Repentance was never yet produced in any man's heart apart from the grace of God. As soon may you expect the leopard to regret the blood with which its fangs are moistened—as soon might you expect the lion of the wood to abjure his cruel tyranny over the feeble beasts of the plain, as expect the sinner to make any confession, or offer any repentance that shall be accepted of God, unless grace shall first renew the heart.

—CHARLES H. SPURGEON

Laws and principles are not for the times when there is no temptation; they are for such moments as this, when body and soul rise in mutiny against their rigor...if at my individual convenience I might break them, what would be their worth?

—CHARLOTTE BRONTË, *JANE EYRE*

No enactment of man can be considered law unless it conforms to the law of God.

—WILLIAM BLACKSTONE

What does it mean in everyday life to be delivered from the Law? At risk of a little overstatement I reply: It means that henceforth I am going to do nothing whatever for God; I am never again going to try to please Him. "What a doctrine!" you exclaim. "What awful heresy! You cannot possibly mean that!" But remember, if I try to please God "in the flesh," then immediately I place myself under the Law.

—WATCHMAN NEE, *THE NORMAL CHRISTIAN LIFE*

If heaven were by merit, it would never be heaven to me, for if I were in it I should say, "I am sure I am here by mistake; I am sure this is not my place; I have no claim to it." But if it be of grace and not of works, then we may walk into heaven with boldness.

—CHARLES H. SPURGEON

'Til sin be bitter, Christ will not be sweet.

—THOMAS WATSON

The office of the law is to excite them to the study of purity and holiness, by reminding them of their duty. For when the conscience feels anxious as to how it may have the favor of God, as to the answer it could give, and the confidence it would feel, if brought to his judgment-seat, in such a case the requirements of the law are not to be brought forward, but Christ, who surpasses all the perfection of the law, is alone to be held forth for righteousness.

—JOHN CALVIN, *INSTITUTES OF THE CHRISTIAN RELIGION*

Though we are commanded to "wash ourselves," to "cleanse ourselves from sins," to "purge ourselves from all our iniquities," yet to imagine that we can do these things by our own efforts is to trample on the cross and grace of Jesus Christ. Whatever God works in us by his grace, he commands us to do as our duty. God works all in us and by us.

—JOHN OWEN

Our faith is a person; the gospel that we have to preach is a person; and go wherever we may, we have something solid and tangible to preach, for our gospel is a person. If you had asked the twelve Apostles in their day, "What do you believe in?" they would not have stopped to go round about with a long sermon, but they would have pointed to their Master and they would have said, "We believe him." "But what are your doctrines?" "There they stand incarnate." "But what is your practice?" "There stands our practice. He is our example." "What then do you believe?" Hear the glorious answer of the Apostle Paul, "We preach Christ crucified." Our creed, our body of divinity, our whole theology is summed up in the person of Christ Jesus.

—CHARLES H. SPURGEON

God has made provision for our holiness. Through Christ He has delivered us from sin's reign so that we now can resist sin. But the responsibility for resisting is ours. God does not do that for us. To confuse the potential for resisting (which God provided) with the responsibility for resisting (which is ours) is to court disaster in our pursuit of holiness.

—Jerry Bridges, *The Pursuit of Holiness*

This life, therefore, is not righteousness, but growth in righteousness; not health but healing; not being, but becoming; not rest, but exercise. We are not now what we shall be, but we are on the way; the process is not yet finished, but it has begun; this is not the goal, but it is the road; at present all does not gleam and glitter, but everything is being purified.

—Martin Luther

Grace means undeserved kindness. It is the gift of God to man the moment he sees he is unworthy of God's favor.

—Dwight L. Moody

Grace means that God does something for me; law means that I do something for God. God has certain holy and righteous demands which He places upon me—that is law. Now if law means that God requires something of me for their fulfillment, then deliverance from law means that He no longer requires that from me, but Himself provides it.

—Watchman Nee, *The Normal Christian Life*

The uses of the law as a rule of life are most efficient means of promoting steadfastness and consistency. Being "written in the heart," it affords to the Christian a *continual touchstone of sincerity*. He has "the testimony of his conscience," that he "consents to the law that it is good"; that he "delights in it after the inward man"; that he "esteems all God's commandments concerning all things to be right"; that he counts his want of perfect conformity to it the sin of every moment; that he is satisfied with no attainment short of being "holy, as he that hath called him is holy," and "perfect, as his Father which is in heaven is perfect."

—Charles Bridges, *The Christian Ministry*

A rigid matter was the law,
demanding brick, denying straw,
But when with gospel tongue it sings,
it bids me fly and gives me wings.

—Ralph Erskine

It is a great mistake to give to a man who has not been convicted of sin certain passages that were never meant for him. The law is what he needs.... Don't offer the consolation of the Gospel until he sees and knows he is guilty before God. We must give enough of the law to take away all self-righteousness. I pity the man who preaches only one side of the truth—always the Gospel and never the law.

—DWIGHT L. MOODY, *PLEASURE AND PROFIT IN BIBLE STUDY*

The law can only chase a man to Calvary, no further.

—DWIGHT L. MOODY

Ignorance of the nature and design of the law is at the bottom of most religious mistakes.

—JOHN NEWTON

So far from law and grace being enemies, they are mutual handmaids: the former reveals the sinner's need, the latter supplies it; the one makes known God's requirements, the other enables us to meet them. Faith is not opposed to good works, but performs them in obedience to God out of love and gratitude.

—A. W. PINK, *A STUDY OF DISPENSATIONALISM*

The law detects, grace alone conquers sin.
—Saint Augustine Of Hippo

Grace binds you with far stronger cords than the cords of duty or obligation can bind you. Grace is free, but when once you take it, you are bound forever to the Giver and bound to catch the spirit of the Giver. Like produces like. Grace makes you gracious, the Giver makes you give.
—E. Stanley Jones

This distinction [between law and gospel] must be observed all the more when the Law wants to force me to abandon Christ and His Gospel boon. In that emergency I must abandon the Law and say: Dear Law, if I have not done the works I should have done, do them yourself. I will not, for your sake, allow myself to be plagued to death, taken captive, and kept under your thraldom and thus forget the Gospel. Whether I have sinned, done wrong, or failed in any duty, let that be your concern, O Law. Away with you and let my heart alone; I have no room for you in my heart. But if you require me to lead a godly life here on earth, that I shall gladly do. If, however, like a housebreaker, you want to climb in where you do not belong, causing me to lose what has been given me, I would rather not know you at all than abandon my gift.
—Martin Luther

# Notes

## INTRODUCTION | A PEOPLE OF LAW AND GRACE

1. Luke 15:11, emphasis added.
2. Luke 15:12, emphasis added.
3. Rod Parsley, *The Cross* (Lake Mary, FL: Charisma House, 2013), 49.
4. Luke 15:13, KJV.
5. Romans 6:16, TPT.
6. 1 John 2:16.
7. BrainyQuote, "F. Scott Fitzgerald Quotes," accessed June 6, 2018, https://www.brainyquote.com/quotes/f_scott_fitzgerald_100572.
8. Clark Whitten, *Pure Grace* (Shippensburg, PA: Destiny Image, 2012), 22.
9. Anthony A. Hoekema, *Saved by Grace* (Grand Rapids, MI: William B. Eerdmans, 1989), 228.
10. Dietrich Bonhoeffer, *The Cost of Discipleship* (New York: Touchstone, 1995), 44–45.
11. Exodus 21:5–6.
12. Psalm 40:6.
13. Matthew 4:19.
14. Isaac Watts, "Alas! and Did My Savior Bleed?," 1707, https://library.timelesstruths.org/music/Alas_and_Did_My_Savior_Bleed/.

## CHAPTER 1 | THE SPECTRUM OF LAW AND GRACE

1. 1 Corinthians 6:18, GW.

## CHAPTER 2 | MEMENTO MORI

1. Hebrews 12:2–3.
2. Philippians 2:5–8.
3. 1 Peter 2:24, NIV.

4. Psalm 22:17–18, NIV.
5. Psalm 22:13, NIV.
6. Matthew 16:24.
7. 1 Corinthians 2:2.
8. 1 Peter 2:24.
9. Galatians 2:20.
10. Romans 6:23.
11. Elisabeth Elliot, *Shadow of the Almighty* (Peabody, MA: Hendrickson, 2008), 144.
12. James 4:4, GW.

## CHAPTER 3 | SOLA GRATIA

1. Roland H. Bainton, *Here I Stand: A Life of Martin Luther* (Nashville: Abingdon Press, 2013), 7.
2. Bainton, *Here I Stand*, 7.
3. Bainton, *Here I Stand*, 18.
4. Bainton, *Here I Stand*, 30.
5. Bainton, *Here I Stand*, 40.
6. Bainton, *Here I Stand*, 44.
7. Bainton, *Here I Stand*, 45.
8. Bainton, *Here I Stand*, 46.
9. Bainton, *Here I Stand*, 51.
10. Martin Luther, "A Mighty Fortress Is Our God," trans. Fredric H. Hedge, 1527, http://www.hymntime.com/tch/htm/m/i/g/mightyfo.htm.

## CHAPTER 4 | WHAT SEEMS GOOD TO THE HOLY SPIRIT

1. Acts 13:46–47.
2. Acts 15:1.
3. Acts 15:21, EXB.
4. Romans 13:10, AMPC.
5. Matthew 22:36–40, TLB.

## CHAPTER 5 | THE LAW AND THE CROSS

1. Colossians 2:16–17.

2. Hebrews 10:1–2.
3. Hebrews 7:11–12.
4. The New Testament does not abolish the Sabbath, but broadens it out into a larger and spiritual "Sabbath rest" (Heb. 4:9–11). It also leaves the question of one day being holier than another to each believer's conscience. Romans 14:5–6 tells us, "One person considers one day more sacred than another; another considers every day alike. Each of them should be fully convinced in their own mind. Whoever regards one day as special does so to the Lord" (NIV).
5. Matthew 5:27–28.

## CHAPTER 6 | THE HEART OF THE MATTER

1. Romans 8:29, NIV.
2. Jeremiah 31:31–34.
3. Psalm 119:41–48.
4. Psalm 119:11.
5. Ezekiel 36:26–28.
6. Romans 3:28, 31.
7. Romans 8:3–4.
8. Romans 8:5–7.
9. Romans 10:4.
10. Galatians 3:24–25, NIV.
11. Christian Smith and Melina Lundquist Denton, *Soul Searching: The Religious and Spiritual Lives of American Teenagers* (New York: Oxford University Press, 2005), 118.
12. H. Richard Niebuhr, *The Kingdom of God in America* (Middletown, CT: Wesleyan University Press, 1988), 193.
13. Jon Butler, Grant Wacker, and Randall Balmer, *Religion in American Life: A Short History* (New York: Oxford University Press, 2011), 278.
14. Jude 3.

## CHAPTER 7 | CONDUCT THAT PLEASES THE LORD

1. 1 Corinthians 8:1.
2. Romans 14:15.
3. Romans 14:14.

4.   Romans 14:14.
5.   Romans 14:13.
6.   Romans 14:17–18.
7.   Romans 14:20–21.
8.   1 Corinthians 10:23–24.
9.   Romans 14:1–2.
10.  Romans 14:23.
11.  Romans 14:3–6.
12.  Romans 14:10.
13.  Romans 14:13–14.
14.  1 Timothy 1:19, NIV.
15.  Hebrews 10:22, NIV.
16.  1 Timothy 4:2, NIV.
17.  Romans 9:1, NIV.
18.  1 Corinthians 8:9–12.
19.  Romans 14:5.
20.  Romans 14:23.
21.  James 1:6–8, NIV.

## CHAPTER 8 | GOVERNMENT AND GLORY

1.   Mark 16:15–18.
2.   2 Timothy 2:15.
3.   Isaiah 9:6–7.
4.   Ezekiel 43:1–12.
5.   Exodus 25:9.
6.   Deuteronomy 23:14, paraphrased.

# Other Books by Rod Parsley

*Finale*

*God's End-Time Calendar*

*Gone*

*The Cross*

*Living on Our Heads*